C000271163

MillenniALL

How to claim your future in the Age of the Millennial

SEAN PURCELL

MillenniALL

First published in 2019 by

Panoma Press Ltd
48 St Vincent Drive, St Albans, Herts, AL1 5SJ, UK
info@panomapress.com
www.panomapress.com

Book layout by Neil Coe.

Printed on acid-free paper from managed forests.

ISBN 978-1-784521-67-7

The right of Sean Purcell to be identified as the author of this work has been asserted in accordance with sections 77 and 78 of the Copyright, Designs and Patents Act 1988.

A CIP catalogue record for this book is available from the British Library.

This book is available online and in bookstores.

Printed by TJ International Ltd, Padstow, Cornwall

DEDICATION

To Elliott, who gave me the reason to start the book and
the motivation to see it through to completion.

TESTIMONIALS

"This is a must-read book for anyone who's looking at starting out in business. It's provided me with advice and guidance that has been pivotal in helping me to make a success of my first 12 months in business. If you are a millennial looking for support in launching your business, then Sean is your guy."

Luke Pitkin, CEO and Founder, Sniiper

"Sean tackles the hard truths facing our snowflake generation, while offering an empowering message: together, snowflakes can create an avalanche."

Ethan Spibey, Founder, Freedom to Donate and PROUD Beer

"As an avid reader, I have seen, read and reviewed many books in the last few years. I have found that most of the time, each new book sets out on a mission to rehash some old theory we have read about a million times. Sean's book does the opposite: he works on a niche that is so relevant for both the millennial and the employers employing them, and coaches you. It gave me, as a millennial and as an employer of millennials, a lot of thinking to do! I would highly recommend this book."

Josh Bardsley, CEO and Founder, Avalanche Enterprise

"In this book, Sean does a great (and needed) job of shining a new light on the millennial generation – thank you!"

Perry Power, storyteller and speaker

ACKNOWLEDGEMENTS

I'd like to thank my family and friends for their support while I completed this book, particularly at times when I felt frustrated and wasn't sure whether I would get it finished.

My thanks also go out to those who coach and inspire me. I believe that to be the very best self, you must spend time around those who push you and challenge your way of thinking. If you have ever been a coach or mentor to me, or if I have been part of a mastermind or networking group with you, thank you.

I also want to recognise my clients; you have given me the confidence to continue spreading my message and helped make me a better coach, speaker and (hopefully) writer. I am humbled that you chose me to be on your journey of entrepreneurship and am committed to helping you play your very best game in business and life.

Finally, none of this would have been possible without the help of Mindy and the team at Panoma Press, whose patience, guidance and honesty has enabled me communicate my message about the potential of the millennial generation further than I ever thought possible.

FOREWORD

I woke up late for a lecture on some day of the week, in some month of the term in 2012. I grabbed my books and bag, got up to campus and made it through yet another hard day reading law. Law. A course I knew I wanted to do from an early age. I had always had a passion for the law, especially family law. My family are givers, in the world of medicine; I believe this rubbed off on me and I too wanted to help people who needed it the most.

I digress. Another day went by, and I woke up to a car horn outside my bedroom window. I realised it was my rowing team. I quickly put my rowing gear on, grabbed a gift I'd made for my team and we hit the river. It was race day and I handed out my gift: handmade rowing socks that I'd put together to help my team bond. We were all short for rowers, and usually got ripped for that. Although we didn't win the race, we did much better than usual – well, that's what our cox said anyway. What took me most by surprise was being approached by a group of other teams, wanting these handmade socks in their sports colours. This was the point when my life was going to change forever. You might be asking, "Why is this relevant?" You will see how this pleasant mistake led to me launching one of Britain's fastest-growing clothing brands, as well as becoming a renowned retail entrepreneur in the US and Europe.

As you are about to read in this powerful book, I am a late-phase-millennial. What does this mean? Well, you will find out what this means shortly, but what does it mean for me? I grew up with the internet. My brother hounded me with stories of how different playtime for me was. I am a millennial through and through. I prefer spending my money on experiences rather than physical things. I like to buy nice clothing as opposed to quick fashion clothing. I find it hard to save, as I am easily tempted to spend money with open, unique and transparent brands and companies – the list goes on. But I am your typical late-phase millennial or snowflake. This being said, my work ethic is my religion. The advice I offer my Hive network (a free group of startup entrepreneurs in London that I meet with every month), the transparency of sharing my life, meetings and progress over Instagram stories, my day-to-day activism and the privacy around my charity work – to me, all of this is a need, as opposed to a want.

Like many other millennials, I feel unrepresented in many industries, especially politically. It is why my generation is the generation of builders. We are being left a terrible economy, with terrible poverty records, and all we want to do is make the world a better place, more advanced, with better communications. It is fair to say that if no one is looking to offer, a millennial will build it for themselves. This is why it has been easy to cast judgments about millennials by calling them disruptors or challengers. The fact of the matter is, if you ringfence and ignore an entire generation, they will do it for themselves. And this is why I am proud to be a millennial.

Risking it all, for what? When I took the decision not to go to bar school after my degree, this was one of the scariest things I have ever done in my life. Everyone, including my family, were telling me not to. I did it anyway, after finding an empty shop in my hometown of Bath, Somerset. I put the money I had been saving since I was 14 years old and opened this temporary shop for seven weeks, to test my idea. Rupert and Buckley Clothing Co opened its doors and we got selling. I was learning every step of the way. I was learning about clothing factories, cash register providers, commercial refuse collections: everything you don't have to worry or even think about as a customer. However, I knew one thing. I was my own boss, and I was the only person who could make this work if I wanted to raise investment, grow the team and grow the company effectively.

What I knew was that I was doing it my own way, a new path untouched. I was risking it. Everyone around me knew I was risking it all. I didn't have the full support of everyone, and just had to make it work.

What I say, after reading Sean's wonderful approach of explaining the dynamics of a millennial, and their perspective and outward view, is that it helps shape what kind of founder you want to be. As a millennial, you are already more risk-positive, you already know that you have to be thrifty, be creative and build – while the media and other generations shower our generation with negatives. Take these and turn them into positives for our generation. We are fast becoming the generation with the highest number of self-made millionaires, and soon will have a higher average working salary than any other generation (not including the 1%, of course).

Take what little our generation has been given, put that to the side. Take your bare, innate skill and prepare it, but then prepare for the hardest bit: taking the first step towards risking it, and the lack of support you may get around you, will be your biggest and hardest challenge. I now help mentor 300 startup founders in London, I share advice on my Instagram @jbuckleythorp, and work one-to-one with startup brands; I understand the journey is untold and varied. This can be worrying, but after a while, it will become normal and exciting, and you will realise you don't have a 'job' anymore, but do what you love, which is your subconscious job. I am just as excited to hear about your journey as you are about starting it. Starting with understanding yourself and your generation is great preparation for becoming a better millennial and a better startup founder.

In this book, Sean has captured the essence of what it is to be a millennial and uses his own experiences and those of others to give perspective. This book is a call to arms, and one that is long overdue.

James Buckley-Thorp,
Founder of Rupert and Buckley,
Forbes 30 under 30 Finalist 2019,
Entrepreneur of the Year 2018

www.jamesbuckleythorp/com

CONTENTS

INTRODUCTION

I remember it very clearly.

I was asked to take on a temporary appointment as curriculum manager for Humanities and Business at a local further education college where I taught. I was in my first full year out of university, had landed a full-time lecturing job after doing it for a few hours a week in my last year of study, and thought it would be a good place to work while I decided how to progress my application to join the Royal Navy as a warfare officer.

I thought briefly about the offer. They said it was guaranteed only until the end of the academic year, that it would give me a significant temporary pay rise, and that it would allow me to test my managerial capabilities.

However, I inherited what felt like the most challenging staff in the department: people who had been in post for many years, who had fallen out of love for teaching, and who certainly didn't have any interest in following a young upstart who wanted to introduce new ways of enhancing the learner experience.

Following another fraught situation (of which there were numerous during this time) where I had attempted to get one of my staff to recognise that they could not behave in their class the way they did, I was on the receiving end of a loud pronouncement, "I will not take any lectures from someone barely out of nappies," by this individual in front of dozens of students, all of whom were only a matter of years younger than me.

I wish I could tell you that my comeback was immense, that I delivered a form of words so well crafted, so profound and yet so cutting that he immediately realised his error.

I didn't.

It wasn't.

He didn't.

Instead I slipped away, chastened and feeling unworthy, believing that his years of physical presence in the building trumped my desire for change and improvement. As the months went on, I felt frustrated, but that changed when I took the opportunity to quickly build a coalition around me of lecturers who got what I wanted to achieve.

Young, dynamic people, they too were recently out of university and wanted to help shape a future for all our learners, to unleash the creativity and potential that is found within each of our learners. They felt that status was earned on merit rather than time served, saw technology as an enabler rather than a barrier, were impatient for change and improvement and were intolerant of mediocrity.

As I grew in confidence and moved from organisation to organisation, I began to challenge the status quo, asking why things had to be done in a certain way just because someone else had said so, exploring what a future full of possibilities could be like, and breaking old-fashioned processes when I found them insufficient for the challenges of the future.

Did it make me unpopular? With some, yes.

Did I continue to hear criticism and a view that I should know my place? Absolutely.

Did I stop moving forward? No way. I knew that there was a generation of people who wanted to be able to make their mark, to have their say, and to have their say heard and respected.

It was then that I became passionate about understanding our journey as a generation.

Every generation has a different environment in which they grow up, and in which they operate as adults.

Every generation comes under criticism and pressure from the previous one and millennials are no different.

However, what concerned me was the speed at which many of us in the millennial generation accepted criticism and attempts to put us in our place. We have allowed people to claim either that a whole generation cannot be stereotyped (which is not actually what people do when they look at generational trends anyway), or that the millennial generation is somewhat less robust, more sensitive and delicate, and naïve.

The millennials I have had the pleasure of knowing, working alongside, and leading in various commercial, not-for-profit, and voluntary organisations could not be further from this caricature.

Very little angers me easily, but when I tell people that I coach millennial business owners and leaders, many take that as permission to tell me everything they believe to be wrong with the millennial generation and, on occasion, to question my judgment for working with them.

I remember one situation where I was on the defensive at a networking event, trying to explain why millennials weren't the weak, overly sensitive, lazy individuals that this person believed them to be, and losing my patience. I decided that I had had enough and began to list all the challenges that the millennial generation faces, all the problems left for them by previous generations that they would need to try to resolve, and all the examples of warmth, intelligence, passion, creativity and hard work that I had seen in those that I had coached and mentored over a decade.

I knew at this point that I needed to go all out. I needed to use whatever platforms were available to me to demonstrate why people should show the millennial generation more respect and to ensure that other millennial leaders and entrepreneurs had someone who had their back. Throughout my career, there were very few people from my generation who I could turn to for coaching, mentoring or support, and I was determined that others should not go through that experience.

Political and civic leaders will soon be mostly millennials.

Business and economic leadership will soon be provided mostly by millennials.

Consumer trends will soon be driven mostly by millennials.

The millennial generation is coming of age.

No longer is it acceptable to downplay our potential and our contribution.

We are coming of age with clear visions of the world we wish to inhabit and are prepared to do what it takes to ensure it can be realised.

I'm proud to be part of this generation, and I hope that this book will act as a call to all millennials. It is not designed to be the only view, but is written to explore what it is to be a millennial and examine ways of undertaking life's journey in a more focused, rich way.

So if you take nothing else from the book, make sure it is this:

Now is the time to claim the millennial label and own it.

Now is the time to think controversially, to offer alternatives, to dream big, to plan well, and to take massive action.

To your success!

Sean

MillenniALL

CHAPTER ONE:

THE AGE OF THE MILLENNIAL IS HERE

When I am asked to deliver talks on the topic of 'the millennial generation', I always start by being clear about what I consider to be a 'millennial'. There are various classifications, but the one I use (and will use throughout this book) is based on the Goldman Sachs definition, which states that a millennial is any individual born between 1980 and 2000. That may seem broad, but most generations are classified along 15 to 20-year timeframes and the millennial generation is no different. By 2019, the millennial generation will be the largest by size in the UK and is already the largest in the US. This has significant implications for business, politics and society. The advantage of this age definition is that it includes people like me, who are at the early end of this timeframe.

A cursory glance through any literature relating to millennials will throw up descriptors such as 'narcissistic' and 'entitled', and references being made to 'generation Me Me Me'. A check through the annals of time, however, will show similarly disparaging remarks made about previous generations, so one could always argue that it was ever thus:

> The children now love luxury; they have bad manners, contempt for authority; they show disrespect for elders and love chatter in place of exercise.
>
> **Socrates**

> The young have exalted notions, because they have not been humbled by life or learned its necessary limitations; moreover, their hopeful disposition makes them think themselves equal to great things – and that means having exalted notions. They would always rather do noble deeds than useful ones: their lives are regulated more by moral feeling than by reasoning. All their mistakes are in the direction of doing things excessively and vehemently. They overdo everything: they love too much, hate too much, and the same with everything else.
>
> **Aristotle**

What is noticeable about our generation is that we grew up in a time marked by the rise of liberal democracy and market capitalism. During my formative years, I observed the fall of the Berlin Wall, the collapse of the USSR, Big Bang (the sudden deregulation of financial markets in the UK), and the supply of easy money. Even for those who were born in the 1990s, the Iraq Wars, 9/11, and the Arab Spring are significant markers in a narrative of upheaval and a desire for change.

Unlike my parents, I grew up in a time of relative economic and political stability, but my peers and I entered a world of education and employment different from that experienced by previous generations. I was one of the first to pay tuition fees for my degree; I also entered the world of home ownership shortly before the great recession of the late 2000s and ended up with negative equity from my first home and no liquid cash to reinvest in another property, which put me off home ownership for some time.

I also watched as those around me struggled to gain meaningful employment: after years of study and fees, many were experiencing a world in which their degrees were not a key to the door of regular employment with career progression. Skills that had been taught at school were starting to become outdated, being replaced with skills needs that hadn't been anticipated and addressed by the education system. Unlike previous generations, we had been brought up in a time when money was in easy supply, public services were being expanded, and employment opportunities looked good; by the time we became adults, we faced a recession, limited opportunities, and an increasing disparity between what we could earn, what we needed to pay for, and what we needed to save.

The environment in which the millennial generation is assuming dominance is one marked by a rise in debt, stretched public services, a downturn in entrepreneurship, a rise in nationalism, rapid technological change, and a fluidity in identity and sexuality. I speak of 'the Age of the Millennial' and this is that time.

Every generation leaves a legacy to the next and this is our inheritance. We need to ask ourselves the question, "What do we want our legacy to be?" We have approximately 20 years before generation Z, or 'post-millennials' take their place as the dominant generation, so what sort of inheritance do we want to leave them?

My message is simple: we have the skills, talents and attributes necessary to make a real difference.

This generation is confident, aware, considerate, tolerant and full of creativity – and, if channelled correctly, can work to create new and exciting solutions to the challenges that we face politically and economically. This book is designed to do just that. I make no apologies for busting some myths and challenging preconceived ideas. Using examples of millennials who have already made a difference, I aim to show you that with some will, energy and a strong message (with the now-obligatory mastery of social media to push it out), you can make real and lasting change. We are at the start of 'the Age of the Millennial' and this book is designed to fire the starting gun for the process of change. I hope that you run with it and that it encourages you to view the world, and your role in it, differently.

Each generation has its own defining characteristics, born of the circumstances in which its members grew up. Millennials are often characterised as being self-indulgent, self-obsessed, and work-shy; we are often referred to in less than flattering terms. More generous and sympathetic research, however, finds a generation that is marked out for being creative, kind, spontaneous, and less materialistic than previous generations. Millennials are more likely to have a concern for wider social and environmental issues and will often make employment or spending decisions based on such concerns. Data suggests that nearly three-quarters of millennials will spend more money on brands that they believe act in a more sustainable manner (Nielsen, 2015[1]), and 90% of millennials would switch purchasing to a brand that had a cause behind it.

Millennials are more likely to think globally, particularly because of our ability to handle digital technologies that have helped open societies and economies up to more detailed and rigorous scrutiny. The use of technology and social media by millennials did not cause the Arab Spring, but it certainly helped amplify to the world what was happening on the ground. Likewise, the use of technology by African millennials has been credited with ensuring that several elections have been held fairly and the losing candidates held to account where they tried to remain in power.

It would be unwise to categorise a whole generation as having the same characteristics, particularly when factors such as class, ethnicity and geography are considered, but many of the issues facing this generation are exceptional in comparison to those experienced by previous generations.

Millennials are the first generation to be truly comfortable with digital technologies: most own a smartphone and use it for a host of activities ranging from social networking, playing games, watching TV and mobile banking. The rise of such technology has helped millennials develop multitasking capabilities and led to a blurring between 'work' and 'leisure', as most activities can be completed immediately, which could partly explain the need for instant gratification that millennials are often accused of demanding.

Millennials are often self-critical though, seeing themselves and their situation in a more negative light than others do. Millennials believe that they will be worse off than their parents and unlikely to achieve the financial security that previous generations have. A rise in the use of Instagram and similar social media applications to promote success, wealth and a perfect body image has also been linked to disproportionately higher numbers experiencing mental health issues, with more millennials saying that they have experienced or are experiencing depression.

Anxiety and FOMO (fear of missing out) have led to many millennials being dependent on instant communication. Some experience 'phantom phone vibration syndrome', prompting them to check their phone routinely in case they miss a message. Such actions lead to a quick burst of dopamine, a neurotransmitter that unlocks the electric stimulation of the brain's 'reward centre'. For individuals experiencing lower levels of dopamine, the process of checking a phone to see whether a message has come through, a photo has been liked, or a status has been viewed and commented on can give a short burst of satisfaction. This is, however, short-lived, so we continue to seek the hit, by checking again… and again… and again. The presence of dopamine in the brain has been linked to enhanced learning; therefore once a pattern of behaviour has been learned that helps to produce it, it becomes hard to break the pattern.

Try it for yourself. Put the phone away for the next hour and see if you can cope without checking it. If you manage to do this, try again for another two hours. Keep increasing the time and find out at what point you are crying out with curiosity about what may or may not have appeared on your phone screen.

It isn't all bad though. The millennial generation is also marked out by its focus on optimism, positivity and the belief that it can make a difference. Millennials are also more likely to be tolerant and socially liberal, but there is still little evidence that their passion for social causes translates into actively exercising their right to vote.

While the majority of leadership roles in business, politics and society are still occupied by generation X (the generation preceding millennials) and some baby boomers (the generation preceding generation X), a growing wave of millennial generation leaders is coming to the fore.

Within the realm of politics, the Leader of the Austrian People's Party and former Austrian Chancellor, Sebastian Kurz, stands out as the youngest leader of a democratic nation. Having undertaken his first major political role as foreign minister at the age of 27, he made a reputation for himself by rebranding his political party and using the tools available to engage a younger demographic. Often referred to as the 'new Macron', he has put his personal brand at the forefront of his party, preferring to adopt the 'movement' style approach of leaders such as Trudeau and Macron (who could be referred to as xennials, individuals who officially belong to generation X but have millennial tendencies). Kurz has used social media to get across his personal message and reach a wider audience – he has more than 282,000 followers on Twitter and more than 32,000 on Instagram, where his posts portray a dynamic and confident world leader establishing Austria as a European nation of influence. His tactic has been to tap into Austrian millennials' disaffection with the status quo – he recognised that many were at risk of tacking on to the more right-wing Freedom Party and therefore confidently moved his party a bit further to the right to counter this, but in a way that was seen as fresh and not aligned to a traditional left-right divide.

According to Professor Pelinka of the Central European University, "Kurz is successful in selling himself as the man of change – despite being a product of the status quo… His youth has helped him to overcome the contradiction that he as an insider is playing the innovator."

The prime minister of New Zealand, Jacinda Ardern, is another millennial leader of a major nation. Her prior election as leader of the opposition led to the creation of a personal movement called 'Jacindamania' after she pledged to campaign with 'relentless positivity'. The success of the Labour Party in winning back power is in no small measure a result of her personal brand and campaigning style. She has 142,000 followers on Twitter and more than 92,000 on Instagram, where her posts are a combination of campaigning, events and random fun shots that demonstrate a relaxed and confident approach to engagement. Her return to work after just six weeks' maternity leave, while her partner remained at home to care for their child, demonstrates that for some millennials traditional male and female roles are not as powerful as they were for previous generations.

While being at a different end of the political spectrum from Sebastian Kurz, she has deployed a similar tactic: using her youth and telegenic personality to engage with disaffected millennials helped to close the gap between her Labour Party and the National Party.

According to Professor Robinson from Massey University, "Jacinda Ardern has shifted the terrain completely. She is a millennial and has woken a large and dormant group of young voters who have been energised by seeing someone they can relate to."

Her response to the Christchurch terrorist attack in March 2019 is demonstrative of the type of leader she wants to be, and frankly the type leader the world needs, with one commentator saying: "This is what a leader looks like." Her millennial worldview was best described by Suzanne Moore of *The Guardian* who wrote:

'Ardern has moulded a different consensus, demonstrating action, care, unity. Terrorism sees difference and wants to annihilate it. Ardern sees difference and wants to respect it, embrace it and connect with it.'[2]

Critics of both leaders highlight their lack of 'real-world' experience, which demonstrates one of other generations' worst beliefs: that results and rewards should be given to people based on the amount of time served, rather than on their capability and commitment. This is a view not shared by millennials in the main.

In the world of business, a striking dichotomy has arisen: while the prominence of millennial entrepreneurs (or 'millipreneurs') is increasing, possibly due to increased exposure through social media, the actual level of entrepreneurship in the millennial generation is lower than for any other generations in recent times. However, interest in starting a business is high, with people being influenced by television programmes such as *Dragons' Den* and *The Apprentice*, and there are many millennial entrepreneurs who are running successful ventures and are supporting others to do the same.

A host of awards and lists such as *Forbes* 30 Under 30 recognise the work of millennials who are making a difference through new products and services. One such entrant on the *Forbes* list is Simon Crowther, managing director of Flood Protection Solutions Limited, who was inspired to set up his business after his family home was flooded on several occasions. As well as building the multimillion-pound business that he started at 18, Simon has received several awards and accolades for his work. Like many millipreneurs, he infuses his work with a desire to operate in an ethical and environmentally sound way, seeking solutions that harness technology and limit the impact on the environment.

Jack Parsons is another well-known millipreneur. After leaving school at 16 with traditional education and employment options closed to him, Jack spent time working in a recruitment firm. He left to combine his passion for helping young people secure great career opportunities with his entrepreneurial skills by creating YourFeed, a social recruitment firm specifically for the millennial generation. During his time as chief executive, Jack built the brand with a small team of other committed millennials, secured funding for the business and created a movement in the field of millennial careers. Jack is now working on another project to support young people into work by harnessing the experiences and capabilities of other youth organisations to compound results and improve the odds for people under the age of 30.

Like others, Jack has woven his own story and personal brand into his business operations, demonstrating that for many millennial entrepreneurs there is less of a dividing line between business and self and, by sharing openly his business challenges with YourFeed and his mental health matters, that authenticity is critical for the millennial generation.

Another example of a millennial entrepreneur is Ben Francis, 26, who has disrupted the sports clothing industry with his business, Gymshark. Having balanced university study by day with pizza delivery by night, and work on his startup in between, he has created a brand that will soon have an annual turnover of £100m and has already started to build a global presence. Gymshark has used the tool of the millennial generation, social media, to help drive brand recognition and sales, drawing on the burgeoning 'influencer' industry to help target a wider audience.

Not all millennial entrepreneurs are political or business leaders: several individuals have made significant and lasting impacts on society by harnessing the concept of a movement and using social media to promote an idea or challenge a social unfairness. The work of Freedom to Donate and its founder, Ethan Spibey, is an example of the ability of the millennial generation to enact real and lasting change.

Over the last decade in the UK, there has been a significant fall in the number of blood donations, but certain groups of people, including men who have had sex with men in the last 12 months, are specifically excluded from being able to give blood. Evidence suggests that such a ban is outdated, so in 2015 Ethan and a small, committed team started a campaign to get the UK government to review it. They used a movement principle, spreading the message via social media and co-opting high profile individuals from the medical profession and from the gay community to campaign with them. They secured endorsements from all major political parties and LGBTQ+ groups and launched a petition, which attracted significant levels of support. The resulting review recommended a reduction from 12 months to three months, which the government has accepted.

This work will enable previously excluded communities to contribute to a cause (blood donation) to which many feel personally attached. The efforts of Ethan and his team led to a substantial social change that did not require large investment, years of planning or the use of traditional means of exercising influence; this demonstrates millennials' creativity and their power to effect real change.

Ethan hasn't stopped there, his latest project is the introduction of PROUD beer; for every bottle sold, a donation of 20p is given directly to LGBTQ+ charities to help their vital work in tackling subjects such as bullying and promoting sexual health. The statement on the PROUD website, "We believed a business could be created to benefit our community and to provide a platform to showcase and support their awesome work" – offers a clear example of how millennials view the leverage that a great business can bring to tackling a social problem.

We demand transparency and openness

To be able to understand the challenges and opportunities facing the millennial generation, we need to appreciate how society is changing rapidly. Each generation experiences significant changes and for millennials this is no different. The growth of plurality in media content makes it hard to distinguish between what is truth and what is fake. Platforms such as Facebook, YouTube and Instagram have democratised information to such an extent that anyone is able to share their views, opinions and knowledge with the masses.

The increase in online media channels has led to a corresponding decrease in traditional media outlets: newspapers sell fewer printed copies and are actively exploring ways of monetising their content online, or acquiring online media channels to further their objectives. Television programmes are increasingly adopting digital features such as Twitter handles and Instagram accounts. In the past, if an individual wished to have an influence, they needed to have a megaphone and be prepared to 'pound the streets' to push their message. Such messages would remain local, whereas now anyone with a smartphone can upload a snippet of video or audio to share with a global audience.

Democratisation of media content offers great opportunities for the millennial, but also poses risks. As the term 'fake news' takes hold, many people are finding it more difficult to ascertain what is true and what is not, becoming less trusting of media output in the process, and often clinging only to that which is aligned with their pre-existing ideas of right or wrong. There is an irony in liberalised media running the risk of creating more intolerance and deep-seated ignorance. Much of what is produced now is based not upon empirical data or research, but on the pronouncement of an individual or a group dressed up as truth. This causes us to be wary about what we read and view, and blunts our ability to hear more objective opinions and viewpoints.

Organisations such as Facebook recognise that this is leading to a gradual reduction in the engagement levels of its users and are looking at ways to 'restore the balance' (ie promoting the social sharing aspect of the platform once more), by focusing newsfeeds on family and friends rather than paid-for content, and potentially introducing mechanisms to flag stories or posts that are not grounded in any particular truth. Traditionally, Facebook posts have been ranked and scored on the basis of factors such as the number of shares and clicks, but the company is now trying to instil the 'social network' element of the site again by promoting those posts that start meaningful interactions, ie conversation and comments between friends and family members, rather than the comments of random strangers.

Furthermore, Facebook intends to reward 'quality news' by promoting it in a new feed, and attempting to curb fake news. Whether these reforms make a significant difference to how people engage with Facebook, particularly in the light of increased distrust following the Cambridge Analytica scandal, is anybody's guess.

The large volume of data that inundates a business day to day, known as 'big data', is one of the biggest changes we are experiencing today. Data-capturing mechanisms that do not require traditional gathering techniques such as forms and surveys lead to our preferences, dislikes and histories being available for sale. We often grant businesses permission to use our data to help craft a better experience (through the use of cookies, for example), allowing them to build an asset base.

It can be said that we are confused beings: we demand accessibility when it comes to finding out information about others, such as the use of open source information to establish a business and check our competition, but we object to authorities holding information on us. We demand privacy in our online and instant communications, preferring the right to privacy over any other competing interest, while we are giving plenty of information out freely online and often not being too bothered about security settings on our profiles and accounts. When was the last time you checked your privacy settings online?

We are, however, at the beginning of a backlash against social media and all things 'online'. New research[3] suggests a link between depression and the use of social media: people who become reliant upon relationships online, and who follow accounts that project a 'perfect' lifestyle, body image and so on, are more likely to suffer mental health issues. Millennials are increasingly switching off their online accounts and reverting to offline activities and experiences that deepen friendships, relationships and personal wellbeing. Social media platforms have reported declining usage among the millennial generation, considered to be their primary market and are altering their interfaces to reflect this. While being online does give a more global outlook, many new businesses are making a virtue of their 'local' feel, emphasising provenance and personalisation.

New initiatives such as The Business Café, led by Penny Power, one of the founders of online social networking, are designed to bring the offline back to the fore. A cursory look at a local coffee house will demonstrate that while many people work alone and online, they still wish to be in the physical company of others. Furthermore, it can be argued that applications such as WhatsApp are being used to deepen face-to-face interactions, rather than replace them.

Millennials prefer to spend their money on experiences, not things

Unlike previous generations, millennials are more likely to spend their money on experiences rather than physical possessions. When I mention this at my seminars, people say to me, "How come I have an iPhone if I'm not interested in possessions?" My reply is simple, "What do you use your phone for? Is it to simply text and call?"

"No," is usually the response, followed up with answers such as, "Twitter, Instagram and LinkedIn," (social media messaging, media creation and curation – an experience); "Tinder or Grindr," (dating applications – an experience); "Banking apps," (personal finance, paying bills, looking at account balances, applying for cards and loans – an experience); "iTunes," (playing music, curating playlists – an experience); "BBC iPlayer and Sky Sports," (watching television – an experience). At this point they usually get the message.

Why are millennials more focused on experiences rather than possessions? Several factors explain this phenomenon. First, it is true to say that millennials are more interested than previous generations in immediate gratification. After all, they have been brought up in a world that is highly visual and immediate. Their parents belong to a generation that saw greed and material wealth as good and often replaced face-to-face parenting with television or computer games, rather than traditional activities, and this has been passed down to their millennial children. Easy credit and a rise in consumerism meant that parents didn't foster patience and deferred gratification in their children.

> You want a PlayStation? No problem, we will buy it now on a credit card and you can have it.

> You want the latest trainers to keep up with your friends? No worries, we can buy it using a store card.

> You want a car on your 18th birthday? That's fine, we can take out finance to pay for it.

Television is now on demand and programmes can be downloaded series by series, rather than episode by episode, which encourages binge watching. Thirty years ago, our major television programmes would be aired once a week and this brought a nation together. People would flock to their Christmas Day televisions to see Dirty Den issue his long-suffering wife divorce papers on *Eastenders*, but now you are just as likely to get a cliffhanger during a standard week as you once did in the Christmas special.

If you missed an episode? No problem, you can catch up any time you like.

The nature of shopping has changed too. Gone are the days when most shops and banks closed on Sundays and bank holidays – 24/7 purchases online are the new norm. To encourage footfall, shops have attempted to lengthen their trading days and continue to push for extended trading hours on Sundays.

> Fancy pizza tonight but don't fancy making it or going out for it? No issue – just go on to your favourite app, create the pizza you crave, and receive it fresh and hot at your door within 30 minutes!

> Want to buy items for your house without changing out of your pyjamas? No problem – just browse Amazon, click a couple of times, and expect it to be delivered within a day.

> Want to book a holiday but don't want to spend your time browsing through brochures and talking to the staff at the local travel agents? No worries – just go online, search for a location, read the reviews, watch

the videos, pop your credit card details in, and your holiday is booked!

Want to meet a potential date without the hassle of going out with mates to a local bar or club? Easy – open your preferred dating app and swipe left and right to your heart's content!

Is it any wonder that previous generations (who in many cases were responsible for creating these easy platforms) have fostered a sense of immediate gratification in the minds of many millennials?

I believe that this sense of immediacy is a natural result of the way we have changed how we live our lives and that there is no shame in living a life that prefers immediate gratification. This does not mean that millennials cannot defer their gratification, however, as shown by the examples of millennial influencers I listed earlier.

A client of mine recently spoke of how significant events in his life had caused him to reflect and recognise that he needed to live a life that aligned with what was important to him; that there was nothing to be gained by being heroic or a martyr or deferring what was important because of the opinions of others. He believes that every time he has made an immediate decision based on what he felt was right for him it has always led to the best outcome.

The preference for buying experiences rather than things is also linked to an increasing sense of despondency that many millennials experience: a feeling that they will never be able to own their own property, start a family or save for the types of material possessions that their parents owned has led to the idea that money should be spent on creating lasting experiences that may never be replicated. There is a growing reluctance to spend significant sums on owning material possessions such as homes or cars: many millennials prefer to have access rather than ownership, a trend known as the 'sharing economy'.

In a pressured world where expectations are high and digital connectivity is constant, being able to spend money on experiences that take an individual away from it all and allow them to recapture their own feelings of control, endurance and achievement is attractive. The growth of the endurance sports industry, exemplified by companies such as Tough Mudder, shows a desire to work as part of something bigger than oneself and to overcome hurdles and objectives that aren't work-related. The sense of person versus the elements, nature and oneself can be rewarding and gratifying.

As a marathon runner, I can fully appreciate the challenge and excitement that comes from setting a target that requires focus and discipline – arguably, this is where millennials do demonstrate their ability to defer gratification. Millennials who are driving ahead in business recognise the power of experience and are creating businesses based on offering such opportunities for millennial customers. While many believe that the digital space has made millennials less sociable, the truth is often the opposite: millennials are keen on the creation of communities of shared experiences, offline and online.

Tough Mudder started its life as an event that was promoted solely by word of mouth and Facebook, and over the years has grown into a business valued at approximately $70 million. It adopted the idea of creating a movement, developed partnerships that helped establish the brand and used digital media such as YouTube, Facebook and Snapchat to reach global audiences of people who wanted to be able to say that they had participated in a Tough Mudder event.

The growth in subscription-based services is fuelled by the millennial generation, with approximately 70% having some form of subscription-based product or service. Whether this involves media (eg Netflix), cosmetics and grooming (eg The Close Shave Society) or food (eg graze), the subscriptions economy is of growing importance for millennials. This isn't just for the product or service itself, but for experience – many of these subscriptions come with a backstory and information about the product, presented using colours and styles that make the process of opening the product a joy in itself.

Spending money on attending sporting events, concerts, cultural activities, retreats and other experiences are seen as far more valuable and enriching than simply owning a possession. For many millennials, happiness is derived from being able to be part of something unique or different or impactful. This does not mean that millennials do not seek to acquire possessions – anyone who said that they didn't would not be being truthful – however, the acquisition of items is about more than just ownership. It is the experience or emotion that is attached to them that matters. This is why, even though I will argue later in this book that home ownership is unnecessary, many millennials still do feel aggrieved about not being able to own a home – it is not because of the need to own a home in itself, but the experience and feelings that are attached to home ownership that matter.

MillenniALL

CHAPTER TWO:

YOU HAVEN'T BEEN DEALT A GREAT HAND

Your economic inheritance

The millennial generation is unlike the generations that preceded it. Unlike our parents, we grew up in a period of relative stability and economic growth. They knew the UK as 'the sick man of Europe', with a 'stop-go' economy in the 1960s and stagnation, strikes and three-day weeks in the 1970s. Most of us, however, entered the labour market just as the Great Recession was about to hit; to this day it is still having an impact, with sluggish growth, no wage growth and public services increasingly at stretching point.

National debt is at the highest level ever: over £2tn, equivalent to nearly £32,500 per citizen. The government continues to run a deficit (meaning that it spends more than it receives). It is estimated that the national debt increases by more than £5,100 a second and little is being done to improve this. Millennials' levels of personal debt and lack of personal savings is troubling. In its most recent 2018 survey, the Money Advice Service found that 55% of all millennials surveyed did not have the minimum recommended safety net of savings: that is, sufficient to cover 90 days' outgoings. The proportion is worse for millennials who rent (65%).

What has driven this? First, the growth in debt accrued for higher education. Millennials were the first generation to experience the financial burden of tuition fees and student loans, unlike their parents, many of whom did not pay to go to university and in many cases were supported by a maintenance grant. When I went to the London School of Economics and Political Science to study Social Policy, I considered the annual fee of more than £1,000 to be high; in most places, this would now be seen as a bargain. While tuition fee levels were modest to start, a sharp increase in the cap (the maximum fee that can be charged by universities), coupled with the removal of maintenance grants for most learners has led to a significantly higher debt burden, averaging £51,000 per student, according to the Institute for Fiscal Studies.

While it is true to say that the loan repayments are not due until an individual has reached a particular income, is relatively cheap credit in contrast with commercial loans and is written off after 30 years if not repaid, this is still debt that sits around the necks, and in the payslips, of millennials across the country.

The reforms introduced by the Conservative and Liberal Democrat coalition government were intended to ease the unfairness of the previous loan system, allow universities to receive generous funding and ensure that loan amounts and repayments were linked to income. The system was designed to create variable student fees, generate competition in the higher education market and link earning potential to degree costs. However, most universities increased their fees to the highest possible rate, irrespective of the earning potential associated with a given degree. This means that many millennial graduates are accruing five-figure debts for degrees that may give them little or no financial advantage. The gradual rise in the number of people undertaking apprenticeships, particularly at higher and degree levels, demonstrates a demand by many to achieve a higher education without incurring costly fees – while receiving an income and gaining valuable work experience. Degree apprenticeships are an increasingly popular option with employers and learners alike.

When I first started as a lecturer in further education in the mid-2000s, I always recommended university to my students. Nowadays my advice is that unless the career they wish to pursue specifically requires a degree, or if the degree they are considering gives strong earnings prospects, or if they really want the university experience and are comfortable with having substantial debt, young people should actively consider alternative options such as apprenticeships. If we do not reconsider our policy on student loans, the UK runs the risk of discouraging many millennials and members of generation Z from applying for university places.

Other forms of debt have increased too, particularly where unemployment, poor employment or low earnings have led to many millennials resorting to credit cards, loans and personal payment plans. Let me be clear, debt is not necessarily a *bad* thing: it can help facilitate purchases of things that we would not be able to afford in one payment, such as a car or a house, or it can help provide a valuable short-term solution to a cashflow issue, for example, through the use of a personal overdraft or a credit card. However, debt is bad when the individual cannot service it (ie make the necessary minimum payments or pay it off), or uses debt to 'credit-surf' (ie moving credit from one balance to another) without using the advantages to pay off debt quicker. The average amount of debt per person in the UK continues to increase daily, and for a millennial this is no different. Accruing debt that doesn't get paid off, or defaulting on payments, can lead to a rapid decline in an individual's creditworthiness, preventing them from accessing further credit.

As stated previously, debt isn't always a bad thing to have, unless you cannot pay it off from your earnings or savings. For a millennial, both of these can be problematic. The average salary has not grown significantly over the last 20 years, but the amount of average debt per person possesses has, thereby increasing the overall debt to earnings ratio.

Most millennials entered the labour market during the Great Recession, when highly paid employment was hard to come by, when there was reduced mobility between jobs and when wage levels remained stagnant. This was different from the experience of their parents, who had largely lived and worked in an era of cheap credit and remortgaging to acquire material possessions, raising their millennial children in a world that encouraged them to acquire things and incur debt: assets such as shares and property would always increase in value, great jobs paying significant salaries would be available, and they would inherit significant sums of money.

Unfortunately, it has become apparent that for many this will not be the case. According to a press release from the Resolution Foundation in 2018, "The UK stands out for having experienced a 'boom and bust' cycle, where strong income and housing gains for postwar generations have failed to materialise for millennials."

When I have written or spoken about this crisis, I have received comments from individuals (usually in other generations) who refer to their own upbringing, tough circumstances, economic issues such as the winter of discontent and the high interest rates of the early 1990s, often suggesting that millennials are somehow more fortunate. Such individuals often talk about 'entitlement', 'selfishness', and the need for millennials to be more patient. Such language is unhelpful and masks the real differences between the economic environment inherited by the millennial generation compared with that of preceding generations: student loans versus free university education; substantially higher house prices in proportion to incomes versus a closer house price to income ratio; home ownership levels at half those of the baby boomer generation; and a higher pay squeeze for millennials compared to members of other generations, who have experienced less pressure on incomes.

Until recently, there has been a view that debt accrued now would be covered by inheritances from previous generations, or by an advance from the so-called bank of Mum and Dad. As previous generations now experience their own challenges, however, many parents are reconsidering whether they can give their children a financial lift. Increased debt, financial support of dependents, pension shortfalls and looming health and social care costs are making people warier about releasing equity for their children, as this may be required in later years.

Research consistently tells us that we are in line for the largest inheritance ever received by one generation from another. Fall rapidly to earth with this fact: you aren't likely to see it until you are about 61.

The longevity of our parents, which in most cases is an absolute blessing, I appreciate, is one factor and requires everyone to receive this wake-up call.

There is no pot of gold waiting for you in a matter of years. That pension you have put off starting won't be topped up with money from Mum and Dad any time soon. That degree debt you accrued won't suddenly disappear.

Your startup business, which could do with a useful loan, is going to have to get used to generating its own cash quickly. (By the way, setting up a business and expecting others to subsidise it for a long period of time means it is not a business: it is a vanity project.)

The inheritance you are hoping for is unlikely to appear when you need it: for example, buying a house, starting a family or investing in a business. Furthermore, the potential inheritance will probably be needed to cover the costs of caring for our parents as they age and require additional support.

So, guess what – unless your parents have plenty of disposable cash, no other children and are happy to downsize significantly, sell their assets or borrow against them, there isn't much coming your way.

This may be a tough message to hear, but it is given with love, from your champion. Don't wait for a handout when you are 61: start earning and saving now. Some millennials will be able to rely upon family to support them and some may benefit from the gift of an early inheritance, but many won't. When you plan for your own financial freedom, don't include any assets that you can see sitting with your parents – you may find that they don't materialise any time soon.

The impact of Brexit

The looming spectre of Brexit hangs heavily over the millennial generation in particular. The majority of millennials who voted in the 2016 referendum cast their ballots in favour of remaining in the European Union and find that they now risk being bounced out of an economic and political structure against their wishes. While I accept the principle that the vote of every individual counts equally, irrespective of the generation they were born into, it is a reality that millennials will have to handle the economic and social consequences of Brexit for longer and in a deeper way.

A significant proportion of the UK workforce at the time of Brexit will be millennials, and millennials make up significant numbers of workers in the financial and professional service sectors, for example, where active contingency planning is being undertaken for a 'no deal' exit from the EU. Millennials could face job losses or relocation to other countries in the EU. Reversion to World Trade Organisation tariffs and rules for exports and imports, or lack of access to a customs union or customs agreement with the EU, will lead to increased prices for consumer products and more difficulty in selling products and services. Furthermore, selling to a club will require adhering to its rules without having any say in the formulation of those rules, Millennial entrepreneurs will need to get a greater handle on the rules and regulations of the EU as a potential customer, rather than the current situation where many of the rules have been influenced by, or are compatible with, the UK.

While it is true that the predictions from some in the Remain camp during the 2016 referendum, for example, that there would be a recession, are looking less likely, it is probable that growth will not be as strong as it would be if the UK remained a member of the EU. Lost opportunities for economic growth will add to the general sluggishness of the UK economy and therefore add pressure on consumers, particularly millennials.

This loss of growth is unlikely to be evenly balanced throughout the UK: localities that were more dependent upon EU investment are likely to see a short to medium-term negative impact on economic growth and social investment. Many EU-funded projects, through mechanisms such as the European Social Fund, will stop and are unlikely to be supplemented by the UK Treasury on a like-for-like basis. This means that a number of social and community programmes will no longer be available, thus reducing the quality and breadth of public service provision in some areas. Education, welfare, health and community cohesion projects are likely to be impacted and these are often the public services that millennials rely on most for support and employment opportunities.

While many people will consider that some economic tightness for millennials isn't a bad thing, the reality is that it impacts upon the whole economy and the financial and social position of other generations too. A contraction in the finances of millennials, who will soon become the largest demographic group in the UK, will have an impact on spending and economic growth. The truth is that younger generations generally spend more than any other and usually on disposable items and experiences; any decrease in purchasing from this group will feed through to the wider economy and slow growth.

There are different types of millennials

For the purposes of this book, I subdivide the millennial category in to 'early phase' and 'late phase'.

Early phase millennials were born during the 1980s and at the time of publishing this book are in their early to late

30s. They are generally embarking on house purchases and the start of a family, and are established in a career or business.

Late phase millennials were born during the 1990s and are starting work or considering higher education. They are likely to be living at home with family or renting property, and attempting to establish their career or first business opportunity.

Any tightening of the financial position for early phase millennials may prevent them from investing in big-ticket purchases such as a family house or car, items that are usually being sold by older generations. By not being able to move out of their first home or rented accommodation, early phasers are blocking opportunities for late-phase millennials to purchase their first property.

The result is that everyone is forced to stay where they are. Property increases in value only when there is a buyer prepared to pay the increased price that a seller demands, therefore any reduction in the ability of a buyer to purchase causes property values to stagnate or fall. The wealth of older generations is often based on property values, and any difficulty in the property market is felt most keenly by these individuals. Therefore, those who argue that a financial contraction for millennials isn't a bad thing are missing the wider point.

Millennials are also entering a very different world of employment from the one experienced by their parents and grandparents. The average length of service with an employer is reducing; millennials are likely to have more jobs during their working life than previous generations did;

and there is a corresponding increase in job insecurity and instability. This is reflected in the growth of the so-called gig economy: individuals contracting with organisations for short-term work, often based around a project, in roles that tend to be temporary and uncertain.

Nevertheless, these are attractive options for millennials. Nearly one in four of those aged 16–30 say that they would consider having gig work in the future (the Taylor review, 2017[4]). The growth in zero hours contracts, which are formal agreements between workers and employers with no guarantee of hours, also impacts millennials disproportionately: over a third of all zero hours contracts are given to those aged 16–24 (Ibid).

The squeeze in pay has not been felt equally across the generations either, with those under 30 in the UK experiencing a contraction at levels seen only in Greece, a squeeze that is disproportionately felt by millennials compared to those in other generations. Pressure on pay is being felt most heavily by millennials, whose need for decent pay is arguably greater than that of older generations, who tend to be more cash-rich and asset-rich.

New arrangements in working practices highlight the volatility and challenges posed by the future of work. Millennials have to view employment in a different way from how it was viewed in the past. The increase in job insecurity is perhaps one of the reasons why millennials are more likely to seek more immediate gratification and progression in employment – if you are unsure whether your job will exist in a couple of years, you are more likely to be demanding of your employer and to seek new avenues in or outside the organisation. It should not come as a surprise to older employers that millennials are less loyal to organisations that are less loyal to them.

Recent media stories highlighted the views of a headteacher at a top fee-paying school who had criticised millennials for lacking 'grit', displaying a sense of entitlement when it came to securing a top job and eschewing many vocational occupations in favour of a 'one-in-a-million' role. He did not blame millennials, rather than the society in which they had grown up, but did say that he felt compelled to speak out when a potential applicant to teach at his school asked why they should come and work for him. This implies a belief that millennials should be grateful for the employment opportunities afforded to them.

There is some truth that an idealised picture of life and what constitutes 'success' has been created through the media. It is also true that many millennials accept lower-paid roles than they had been led to expect would come as a result of undertaking higher education, that many are accepting lower pay to undertake apprenticeship programmes, and that a number of millennials undertake voluntary work and unpaid internships to gain experience. Also, an employment relationship is meant to be two-way; where employer and employee can share value with each other, higher commitment and greater performance usually follows. Therefore, in asking the interviewer to explain why they believe their organisation and opportunity is the best option for the applicant, the interviewee is asking a sensible and understandable question.

Other generations are quick to ask what millennials are doing to improve their lot, but fail to recognise that a lack of stable employment, a growth in the number of graduates who are not able to realise higher earning potential (even though they were told by family members, teachers, and careers advisers from other generations that this was the best route), and a lack of financial capacity to save and build personal assets, is mostly a result of the actions and decisions of non-millennial individuals and institutions run by them. Put simply, the house has been set on fire by other generations who are expecting millennials to put out the fire and then rebuild the house without any materials or labour from them.

Increased living costs and stagnating earnings are putting significant and sustained pressure on individuals and families as they struggle to keep up with day-to-day living costs, even though many are working a substantial number of hours a week. A sad sight is the number of people forced to use food banks to supplement their living; many of those accepting such charitable support are working and earning. Several surveys put millennial poverty at one in five, and often higher than any other generation. Furthermore, poverty now can lead to poverty in the future – if millennials remain poor for a considerable period, they are unlikely to be able to gather the assets and make the savings needed to prevent poverty as pensioners. Above-inflation rises in the cost of foodstuffs and other essentials for millennial families, such as childcare, have locked people in to a spiral of ever-decreasing disposable income, a reliance upon credit and an inability to save.

Changes in employment structures, increased debt, a lack of disposable income, delayed inheritances and an inability to purchase a home are all serious matters that face the millennial generation as they deal with the trials and tribulations of adulthood. The compound nature of these barriers and challenges was brought home to me sharply when I received a comment on a post I had written on LinkedIn relating to the latest data on housing and the millennial generation from an individual who wrote the following (anonymised for this book):

> At 32 I have absolutely zero chance of buying a property any time soon. My husband has a chronic disability ... and so would limit our mortgage options, plus he's 20 years my senior, so would limit those options further. We have no savings, largely due to the fact that having two children under 4 have forced us to pay in excess of £1.4k per month in childcare costs, leaving us no room at all to put anything aside. Looking on the BBC today, if I use their calculator to work out what I can afford, I either move to the most northerly region of Scotland ... or, if I stay in my current region, I have to have a deposit of £60k and a monthly mortgage payment of at least £1.1k to afford anything. It's impossible, so I have resigned myself to the fact that I will always rent (unless I win the lottery or 'come into money'). A number of my friends who have bought houses, despite having good incomes, have only been able to do so through gifts from family, loans from parents or even inheritance from when a relative has died. It's a really disheartening situation.

While not reflective of all millennials, this is a narrative that is all too familiar. What a tragic situation for many to find themselves in.

Such an environment has caused a shift in relationships and there is some evidence that the nature and structure of relationships are changing as a consequence of economic and social pressures. The average age of those entering into a committed relationship is increasing, the age of those individuals choosing to marry or enter a civil partnership is increasing, and the average age of a couple choosing to start a family is on an upward trend. While the intensely personal and emotional nature of relationships is not always determined by economic factors, a rise in job instability, an inability to save meaningfully and a need to chase an increasingly limited pool of professional, career-building jobs by working harder and longer (#hustle) means that time devoted to finding intimacy and love is seen as time wasted. As one millennial put it to me recently:

> I was recently looking for a new job and one thing that struck me was how lucky I am at the moment; I have no girlfriend/wife/children who I need to think about when moving jobs/location. I have no mortgage that I need to worry about, just a tenancy that requires two months' notice. This made me … more attractive to employers as I was willing to relocate if necessary, even considering jobs in Paris for a while.

If we are the generation that is officially the most 'stressed', as suggested, the most 'experience-driven', the most 'now-centred' and the most financially insecure, this would help to explain the choices that millennials now make when entering the world of dating and relationships.

As the first generation to have grown up with technology that can be used to replicate, enhance or replace relationships, we have grown accustomed to apps and software that can help us cut down on the stop-start nature of old-fashioned dating. In the past, we would have had to go out with friends for dinner, a trip to a bar or a club, and then possibly indulge in some flirtatious conversation with a stranger about whom we felt strongly enough to arrange a 'date'.

If we were not social butterflies, we would have met someone through work, or a sports club, or a hobby, or in a particularly barren period, been subjected to speed dating or a blind date arranged by friends. Any of these options meant that we met someone in the flesh, we heard their voice, we saw how they dressed, stood and behaved. We would also be able to chat with their friends who were out with them, in a poor attempt at a character reference (did we genuinely ever think that their friends would say anything other than the positive?). A formal meetup at another time would allow us to get to know each other, to ask questions and hear an answer and see a physical response, and this would allow us to decide whether we wanted to progress any further. However, this is time-consuming, potentially expensive and not necessarily any more 'honest' than other dating approaches – are we really of the view that people would put out their authentic selves in the first few encounters?

Dating has become quicker, cheaper and potentially more sophisticated. From the comfort of the train home, the work desk, the gym or the bedroom we are able to search for people based on a range of factors and permutations: hair colour, height, love of classical music, sexual preferences, wealth – each of these we can find out about without having to awkwardly introduce it into conversation over the dinner table at a restaurant; we can find out what type of relationship they are looking for – a quick hook-up, a relationship, marriage and children; we can also find out how close they are to us at the exact moment we are searching and whether they want to meet someone there and then.

Accessibility? Tick.

Ease? Tick.

Lack of awkwardness? Tick.

Avoidance of painful and abortive first dates? Tick.

Cheap? Tick.

Authentic? Hmm…

The difficulty with such online apps is that we are taking a chance that the information, images and person being presented are true and authentic. If they are (and many are), then happy days; if they are not, then this could present itself as something between mild irritation over deception through to real danger, but is it any more dangerous than meeting someone in a club, barely having a meaningful conversation and then going home with them?

Once millennials get beyond the stage of dating and enter the world of committed relationships, they may find that economic pressures limit their ability to fulfil all the hallmarks of a long-term relationship that their parents perhaps enjoyed. Some will find that they cannot move in together, due to the cost of renting, and have to continue living with parents or flat-sharing with others. Those who can rent may find that their capacity to save for the purchase of a home, marriage, or children is limited, forcing them to stretch financially beyond their means or delay these commitments in the hope that their financial situation improves.

The millennial generation is comfortable with technology and the use of social media, but this has begun to create what I call a 'curated life'. By our nature, we seek to present our very best selves to the world and social media platforms allow us to curate our day to day life, amplifying great times and positive experiences, and pushing the acquisition of possessions. Pressure to conform is felt most by teenagers, but is still present in cohorts of those in their 20s and 30s – expectations are driven hard by society and previous generations, and this is exacerbated by the 24/7 nature by the digital world. Constant selfies and posts offer only one aspect of our lives, which therefore presents a misleading picture to others about the lives we lead. Anecdotal evidence from plastic surgeons suggests a rise in the number of millennials booking in for surgery – it would seem that selfies have made people conscious of the size of their noses!

The demand to obtain a career and to 'make something of yourself', the pressure to hit the ground running and make significant revenue when starting a new business, the push to find 'the one', fall in love and start a family, the gentle hints to move out of home, the constant messages to eat in a certain way, exercise in another way, drink more water, drink less alcohol, drink more alcohol, to #hustle – these messages are introduced by family and friends, amplified by wider society, pushed hard by traditional media and marketing channels, and compounded by relentless social media. It is no wonder that we are the stressed generation, experiencing higher levels of disconnect and an increase in the incidence of mental health issues that are recognised and diagnosed.

Increasingly, millennial celebrities and other well-known individuals are talking about their own pressures and how they are tackling or have tackled depression. In 2017, Stormzy spoke candidly about his battle with depression, powerfully talking about how he thought that this was something that 'strong' people didn't experience, but that he knew even those who seemed strong and successful were often facing their own challenges. Here, social media has been a powerful tool in helping raise the issue of poor mental health within the millennial generation and it has made many people feel comfortable about acknowledging their challenges.

For my own part, I was diagnosed with depression in January 2017 after a period in which I could not face up to the difficulties I was experiencing as I tried to juggle a range of pressures. I took medication for quite some time and have altered my lifestyle to improve my wellbeing, but not until recently would I have felt comfortable with people outside my immediate family knowing. The rise in other entrepreneurs talking openly about their mental health issues has made me feel more comfortable about owning my own condition and supporting others in managing theirs. As with most things in life, social media can be a tool for good as well as bad.

So:

The highest levels of national and personal debt to face any generation.

The rise of populism and the uncertainties caused by Brexit.

Delays in the realisation of inheritances.

Fiscal and public service pressures caused by needing to support an increasingly ageing population with complex needs.

A rise in job instability and more graduates without access to graduate, high-paid jobs.

A lack of true housing supply, both rental and owned.

An increase in 'perfect' lifestyles promoted on social media leading to a lack of self-confidence and a rise in mental health issues.

An inability to start and sustain intimate relationships.

Sure, the millennial generation does feel entitled, but it is no surprise in a world that has told them that the future looks bright, that they can have it all, and that all should be able to climb the highest heights, yet through poor decisions has saddled it with a more uncertain, disconnected and depressing future. If people question the resilience of millennials, they are wide of the mark – by making demands, by attempting to get ahead, and by seeking to connect with experiences that make them happy and whole, they are proving their potential to be the most resilient generation of all.

MillenniALL

CHAPTER THREE:

EACH GENERATION HAS ITS OWN UNIQUENESS

To understand millennials, how they have developed, why they think in the way they do and the reasons that they behave as they do, it is important to take a little time to review each of the generations preceding the millennial generation and evaluate their impact.

From the turn of the 20th century, there have been approximately four generational cohorts preceding millennials: those referred to as the 'GI generation' (born 1900–24); the 'silent generation' (born 1924–45); 'baby boomers' (born 1946–64); and 'generation X' (born 1965–79). Each had its own challenges and unique environment; each saw work, family, education and social status through the prism of major events or traumas that they experienced; their own world views were shaped, and were largely rejected by the generation that immediately followed them.

Members of the GI generation were old enough to serve in the second world war and major conflicts on either side of it. They were brought up during a period of financial turmoil (the roaring 20s and the subsequent Great Depression), the collapse of many old nations and empires and the surge in extreme political ideologies such as fascism and communism. This generation clung to the 'old order' when class was all-important and social mobility unheard of; for them education was functional for the working classes and the preserve of the middle and upper classes; employment was fixed, and work was to be seen as a duty; and the family was the centre of everything. These individuals also observed the impact of major war – the first world war in particular – on previous generations and also started to see the opportunities afforded by mass production and the film industry.

Members of the silent generation were too young to serve in the second world war, but grew up in the shadow of it, suffering the after-effects in terms of rationing, poverty and the need to rebuild. For these individuals, the greater good was prominent: rebuilding homes, the establishment of a national health service and the expansion of the welfare state all gave a sense of the needs of the wider community over the individual.

Baby boomers feature regularly in today's media coverage, as these are the people who have retired or are thinking of retiring soon. This generation is named so because of the large boom in the birth rate in the late 1940s, following the end of the second world war. This generation is noted for major social, economic and political changes because of improved living standards, the embedding of social welfare and consensus politics. The late 1950s and early 1960s were marked by a sense of positivity, hope and progress, which could be seen in the space race between the west and the east culminating in the first Moon landing. Society also experienced a shift with the rise in recreational drug-taking, a liberalisation of the media, a new sexual awakening, the women's liberation movement and a rebellious streak in the youth of the age, who grew up listening to music genres such as rock 'n' roll. The values of this time were driven by the freedom, experimentation and materialism that was emerging.

Generation Xers grew up during a time of industrial strife, recessions and the height of the cold war. People growing up in the 1970s began to feel the impact of global shocks and to realise how dependent nation states were on each other. The consensus that had been the hallmark of the 1950s and 1960s gave way to division and the rise of new approaches to running the economy, such as monetarism. People of this generation entered the labour market at a time when painful reform had caused significant inequality in communities, classes, genders, and ethnicities, leading to a have and have-not society. Generation Xers experienced a significant financial boost following deregulation of the City of London in 1986 (big bang) and this was supported with laissez-faire economic policies. Consumption and the acquisition of things became the hallmark of this period, with people spending significant sums on new technology, property and other material goods: the more ostentatious, the better. This was the era of Harry Enfield's *Loadsamoney*, the rise of famous entrepreneurs such as Alan Sugar and Rupert Murdoch, and the "greed is good" mantra of the film *Wall Street*. All of this was followed by a painful correction as boom turned to bust, forcing up interest rates, causing businesses to close and properties to be repossessed. The bust was exacerbated by the UK being forced out of the European Exchange Rate Mechanism (ERM) on Black Wednesday (16 September 1992).It took until the mid-1990s for the UK's economy to start recovering from the damage caused by the corrections of the early 1990s.

And so, I come on to the millennial generation. Or do I?

I once delivered a talk on millennials and during the question and answer session, a hand was gingerly raised.

"Yes?" I asked brightly.

"I was born in 1979 and I share a lot in common with millennials, but according to the definition, I'm generation X; surely this shows that the labels can't be applied?"

There were a few nods around the room as those who were born in the late 1970s identified with the question. Someone else spoke up.

"I was born in 1981 and I don't feel like a millennial."

A couple more nods. I smiled and reassured them that this was a question regularly asked and I proceeded to give my answer, which I expand upon below for those of you who would sympathise with these questioners.

There are a group of people (including me) who were born in the late 1970s and early 1980s and are old enough to remember the greed and materialism of the late 80s and early 90s, who can remember the emergence of Tony Blair and the New Labour landslide in 1997 and may have even voted in that election. These individuals can remember mobile phones that were built like bricks; asking people to stay off the phone as they wanted to use the dial-up internet (if you don't know what dial-up internet is, you make me feel incredibly old, even for a millennial); and there being only four television stations. However, they also grew up in a period of technological advancement, and can comfortably and confidently use social media and the web; they were the first to be hit with student loans; they entered the world of work only to find that within a couple of years their personal finance and career planning had gone up in smoke due to the financial crisis; and also found that starting a family and buying a home was out of their league financially.

These are the 'xennials'.

Every generation has a micro-generation that is a little too young for one cohort and a little too old for another – if you have a 3 at the start of your age and even an early 4, then you are likely to be a xennial, or an 'early phase millennial' as I have termed it in this book. This doesn't mean you are not part of the millennial generation, it just represents those that were born in the transitional phase between generation X and generation Y. The best description of a xennial is an individual who had an analogue childhood and a digital adulthood.

Xennials grew up in a world mostly without the internet, when films couldn't be downloaded or streamed but had to be rented from the local Blockbuster store, when computers were large and cumbersome, and choice in television was only beginning to emerge with cable and satellite.

When I was young, we had one 'digital asset' – an Olivetti 286 with a dot matrix printer attached, which whirred in to action and printed on to paper that had perforated edges and punched holes along the side. When I was 13, my nan bought me my first personal computer, so that I could access the internet to do my homework, and an inkjet colour printer. Online research was limited, however, due to the lack of valuable content online and the speed of my dial-up internet. For many years, I continued to trudge to the library to research and used the computer to merely type and design. For me, the most exciting part of my first 'proper' PC was the pack of games I received, introducing me to the colourful (and intuitive) world of Championship Manager and latterly Football Manager, a game I continue to play and download to this day. I bought my first computer from a retailer called Escom, which expanded significantly before going bust in the mid-90s. Other companies, such as Tiny, came and went, particularly as the PC market expanded and players such as PC World came to the fore.

Xennials experienced the excitement of Windows 95, a new operating system that offered a step change in how computers operated, helping to embed Microsoft firmly in the mind. Windows came with games such as Solitaire and Minesweeper, allowed us to browse using Internet Explorer, supported our studies through Microsoft Encarta – a significant programme that required installation using several CD-Roms.

Social media was new for us, and Xennials were the guinea pigs for new ways to stay in touch using technology. We signed up for a MySpace account, added grainy photos of ourselves, followed bands that we liked and tentatively started to find our first online friends who had similar interests. These changes didn't affect just us: baby boomers and generation Xers who had some technological capability signed up for a Friends Reunited account, connecting with people they hadn't seen for decades, since school, sharing photos and stories, and arranging meetups and reunion parties. The internet seemed to us to be a place full of excitement and possibility, if only we would work out how to use it.

As a teenager, I received my first mobile phone – a large, black BT Cellnet mobile with a stumpy aerial that I could personalise by changing the black plastic ring around the aerial for a vast range (four) of colours. It was a pay as you go, and I used to buy a voucher from my local shop, rip it open, scratch a panel and enter a code every time I wanted to add £10 of credit. This was a regular occurrence, as texting was fun, but expensive (10p per text). Others had the latest models – a Nokia in particular held teenagers in rapture as it allowed internet access (of a fashion) and the game Snake occupied an increasing amount of our downtime.

Businesses were also starting to make the gradual change from analogue to digital and this was nowhere more obvious than in the travel industry. As I and other xennials were growing up, the process of buying a holiday required a visit to a travel agency in town, a review of the available brochures, and a long period of waiting while the agent accessed a database to work out availability and cost. It was never a short experience and buying a holiday was often based on the small paragraph in a brochure and the recommendation of the agent if they had been there (in fact, you never actually knew if they had been there or were simply giving a sales line).

Gradually, as the internet allowed for photos, interactive videos and reviews, we were able to conduct significant research online, ultimately buying our dream trip from the comfort of our own home. This became the case in retail, hospitality, recruitment and car sales – everything shifted from the physical and face-to-face to a digital footprint. Xennials were at the forefront of using the first applications, software, hardware and systems; things that later stage millennials would come to take for granted did not exist, and gradually emerged over time for the xennial.

Does this transition from analogue to digital make xennials vastly different from their millennial peers? I don't believe so. While xennials are not quite the digital natives and grew up in a time that predated much of the experience of later-stage millennials when they were approaching their teenage years, there is much that they share, mostly economic and social. As xennials became more digital and entered a labour market and economy similar to that experienced by other millennials, the gulf between them and generation X became more apparent and will continue to widen.

And so, my writing brings me to the millennial generation – a cohort of people who are socially liberal, uncertain yet confident, ambitious yet keen on balance, talented and knowledgeable, but at a great financial cost, wanting to make an impact on the world, but chained to implementing the decisions and fixing the problems of those who have gone before.

A cohort who still believe in love, relationships and marriage, yet put them off until later, who would be prepared to make sacrifices for their business or career ambitions, but have difficulty in securing meaningful employment opportunities.

A cohort who consume the teachings and advice of big business thinkers, who enjoy the #hustle, who look at ways of starting a successful business, but who also are less likely to start a business than any other generation before them.

Optimistic, engaging, resilient in the face of uncertainty, determined, passionate about experiences and causes, full of integrity and the belief that all matter. This is the generation that I see every day in my work as a coach, speaker and trainer, and not the caricature of a 'snowflake' that others would seek to portray.

The first part of this book has focused on the difficulties, the obstacles and the challenges facing the millennial generation as they take their place as the dominant force in business, politics, the economy, and society. The second part is designed as a call to arms – an invitation for millennials to accept the title of 'millennial' and see no shame or value judgment placed upon it. The world is changing and the old ways of viewing things and doing things are slipping away, to be replaced with a new narrative, one that is being shaped by ambitious, intelligent and passionate millennials every day. The book will seek to challenge the old ways of thinking and offer suggestions for a new way, drawing upon examples of those who are changing the world, one tiny piece at a time. You too can do this, and I want you to see this book at your permission to go out and stake a claim for your own future. It is your time: the Age of the Millennial has arrived.

MillenniALL

CHAPTER FOUR:

HOME OWNERSHIP IS NOT THE ONLY WAY

If you are a millennial reading this book, you are likely to be either a have or a have-not when it comes to housing.

Whenever I meet millennials and ask them about their greatest challenge and biggest priority, they often cite their inability to rent or buy a home. Research tells us that the financial obstacles facing millennials are greater than any experienced by previous generations – the gap between annual earnings and the cost of a home is substantially greater than that experienced by older generations. The housing crisis for millennials is the culmination of several structural issues that have created, and locked in, intergenerational inequality.

Many millennials are now assuming greater levels of debt even before they enter the labour market: student loans, private credit and the increase in living costs have all put pressure on millennials even before they have begun to look for work. Once employment is secured, it may be in lower-paid or unpredictable work, as is typical in the gig economy, where people are employed only for specific projects or pieces of work. Lower pay and lack of job security means that the individual's ability to save for a big-ticket item, such as a house, is limited, because living expenses, rather than savings, received priority. It is no surprise that only a small percentage of millennials have saved enough for their rainy days and that many do not have any form of long-term savings, let alone for the purchase of an asset such as a property.

As rent increases, many find it difficult to set money aside for the eventual move into a property, and the hopes of many millennials rest on their parents (or the government) stepping in with a loan (or Help to Buy scheme) to secure the deposit necessary to make the purchase. Even if the deposit is secured, stringent requirements from the mortgage lenders – including employment history, income statements and credit checks – make it hard to find a mortgage that fits the applicant's needs.

The haves are those who can prove a secure and stable income, secure some financial support from family or friends and afford the repayments necessary. I would not have been able to get on the property ladder had it not been for the government's Help to Buy scheme available at that time, which enabled me to buy my first apartment in Essex.

Unsurprisingly, the haves are fewer in number than the have-nots. The have-nots are those who cannot prove that they could make the necessary payments for their own place and, because of low income or a lack of stable income. Many of these individuals do not have parents or family members who can offer financial support for a deposit payment. Furthermore, as many millennials are entering the labour market later and remaining on lower incomes for longer, they are unlikely to be able to make an investment in property until later, possibly in their 40s.

I use the word 'investment' here deliberately.

Part of the problem for millennials is that previous generations have begun to see property as less of a 'home' and more of an investment. For decades, people have been encouraged to view houses as assets that will continue to appreciate in value over time, and this has been at the expense of viewing a property as a home. The rise in buy-to-let, coupled with easy credit for people who already own a home, has led to a system where houses are viewed as another asset for flipping at a profit. This isn't limited to individuals investing in actual bricks and mortar: housebuilders and land developers are as guilty of inflating prices through land-banking (withholding building on land to wait for the value of the land to increase and then sell on), and through seeking to build properties that have a higher sale price.

The amount of land in the UK that is built on is relatively small. The BBC created a neat search engine that can tell you how much land in your area has been built on – go to https://www.bbc.co.uk/news/uk-41901294 and have a look.

I live in a town called Maldon, in Essex: a town with a long and proud history. A drive around the area and the local villages would give you the impression that this is a place where significant housebuilding is taking place, but a review of the data shows that only 3% of Maldon and the surrounding area is actually built on. A proper drive would bear this out: lots of green spaces, fields, woodland and marsh lands. The UK as a whole is not much better, with approximately 6% of the land built on. So, when someone says that there isn't much space to build on, they are referring to urban areas and cities (eg the City of London, 98% of which is built on) and not most of the country.

Another complicating factor in the speed of housebuilding is political – planning permission can be an arduous process involving delays, reviews and a general drive by nimbys to frustrate the process, attempting to prevent their area being covered in concrete, even though it is clear that most of the land has never encountered a drop of concrete and is unlikely to do so.

Put simply, locals will protest, politicians will prevaricate and housebuilders will build when they want and not when it is needed. This is what prevents us building enough houses for everyone. As a result, millennials who want to buy a home are forced to pay inflated prices in areas close to major towns or cities, or near train lines or A roads, or they are hounded out to areas that are cheaper but more disconnected from critical infrastructure.

I am a Dagenham boy by background. For those who don't know where that is, Dagenham is an east London borough on the border of Essex. When I looked to buy my first property, I could not find anywhere that I could afford until I found a development in an Essex town called Witham, approximately 30 miles along the A12 road. The flat was great, the town was up and coming and had all the amenities needed, and it was a short drive from Chelmsford and Colchester.

However, it was approximately an hour-and-a-half drive to work back near where I grew up, and often took anywhere up to two-and-a-half hours to get home, particularly on a Friday afternoon. Having seen a number of streets in Witham deserted during the day, the A12 filled with cars and the train station packed with commuters, it was clear that many of us had moved to the town because of its property costs and were suffering by having to do longer journeys.

On my train journeys into and out of London, I would often catch the train from London Liverpool Street to Norwich and would watch people sitting on a train for the best part of two hours. One commuter I spoke to explained that he worked in the City and lived in Norwich as he had a family and needed to get better value for their money; his sacrifice to ensure that they had a decent family home was to make that journey every day and pray that there would be no delays. What makes this picture more depressing is the thought that as the gap between what we earn and what we can afford expands, the geographic gap is likely to get bigger.

So, faced with these pressures, it is no wonder that millennials have been dubbed 'generation rent', because many of them either rent property for a longer period than previous generations or express a view that when they are able to move out from home that they will rent. The rental market is hotter than ever before, with people either choosing or being forced to rent, which has also led to rent inflation in the most desirable areas.

But is renting always a bad option? From what I have written so far, you would think that it was inferior and unsatisfactory, but it does not have to be so. While affordability is one of the primary drivers for millennials to rent, there are a host of advantages in not entering the property market as an owner-occupier.

1. You may pay a premium, but your risks are reduced

Think about it: as a tenant you have rights that are enshrined in law and the landlord is legally obliged to ensure that your property is of the right standard and specification. If the boiler breaks in your own property, you must pay for it and arrange to get it fixed. In many rented properties, this is the landlord's problem and they must provide a fast way of getting the heating and hot water back on at their own cost. You also don't have to worry about things like replacing windows and doors, wear and tear, and buildings insurance. You pay to rent, and the landlord (should) take care of the rest – assuming they are not a modern-day Rigsby (ask your parents who that is if you are unsure).

2. You have flexibility in tenure

When I owned a property, I decided that I wanted to seek a new job opportunity and also study for a master's degree. I had studied for my first degree in London and lived at home, so didn't have the full 'living away from home' student experience and decided that I would do this as a postgraduate. The problem was that I had a property with a mortgage that needed paying, so I had to rent it out temporarily. I then stayed in my new job for longer than anticipated and had to extend the rental period; finally, when my mother was diagnosed with cancer, I moved closer to support her and still needed to rent the property out. It was at this point that I decided to sell.

At the wrong time in the market. After repayment to the bank, plus an early repayment charge and legal fees, I walked away with very little to show.

Not owning allows for far more flexibility in where you work and for how long you work at that place. Want to move? No worries: just give the landlord the required notice and arrange for your furniture to be sold or removed. As one of my clients said, "Renting means I can take my business and my career anywhere; I now know that I can live and work anywhere I like at short notice, which makes me a far more attractive prospect to employers and investors."

Ask yourself: is it worth it?

Those who talk about property being worth it are those who view it as an asset, and this is of course true, but a house or apartment is meant to be more than that: it is meant to be a home.

A bastion of security and safety, a place to live, to love, and share experiences, and not simply a financial transaction. Like many assets, property can fall in value as well as rise, and these fluctuations are not uniform – if property is always an appreciating asset, then why do some places in the UK experience very limited growth in value? Is it really worth someone slaving away for 30 or 40 years, making improvements to their property, if in real terms it isn't much more valuable than before?

What are you actually buying it for?

Congratulations, you have bought your own home.

Although it isn't your own home, as you put 10 or 15% or so in as a deposit and borrowed the rest.

Most of the home is owned by the bank, and in the first couple years your mortgage payments cover only the interest accrued.

But you do it. You keep plugging away, repaying your mortgage and making bigger repayments to try and reduce the duration and total amount repayable.

Then someone tells you it is worth more and if you sold it, you could realise some nice profits, which would help you buy that bigger home that you now need. So you do it.

But the rest of the market has also increased in value, so your profit isn't getting you much further.

And you have a bigger mortgage to pay.

And you pray that the interest rates won't go up, as the repayments are now at the edge of what you can afford.

Congratulations, you are now fully paid up. It has taken you the best part of 40 years to get there, but you have done it.

But your pension isn't worth much, and you would like to travel and also give yourself a little income, so you look at some form of equity release or downsizing.

And then you get a bill for the social care you need, and your property is sold to pay for it. Unless you were acute and took financial planning advice, you hadn't prepared for this and you leave those behind you with very little. That home you had worked all your life to pay for has gone, with not a lot left to show.

But CONGRATULATIONS, you owned a home!

Does it really have to be that way?

Renting can allow you to live in the property you want and can afford, often on long-term tenancies, but also with the flexibility to move if circumstances dictate. You can channel your disposable income into other investments for the future, rather than spending it on an asset that you hope will add value for that time when you need to turn it into cash and to give someone else. Indeed, renting is a popular option in mainland Europe where stable rents, good provision of rented housing supply and a cultural acceptance of renting allows this to be an affordable option.

Am I suggesting that owner-occupation is bad? Of course not. I own my property, but I am acutely aware that I am one of the haves. For the have-nots, society should not pressure people into home ownership and should work to ensure that there is a fair supply of decent rented accommodation, so that people can rent for longer periods until they are ready (and I stress *until they are ready*) to invest in property. It is true that few people want to rent forever and that a property is seen as an asset class in the UK because of repeat booms in prices, encouraging people to view their home as a long-term savings plan; but this does not mean that a solid supply of decent, affordable rented accommodation should not be a government policy priority.

When millennials are ready to enter the property market, a range of incentives and financial packages are available to ease that transition. Increasingly, the Help to Buy scheme has been touted as a way to help millennials to secure their first property, with the state taking a stake in the property in return for equity or rental contribution. There has been high demand for the scheme, but I have two primary concerns:

1. Encouraging millennials to move back to 5% deposit schemes is arguably the exact thing that helped cause the last crash.

2. The loans require monthly service charges, which are linked to inflation, meaning that many millennials could find themselves with a bill of a few thousand pounds extra a year; financial pressures could lead to the homeowner needing to sell while the equity in the property is negative.

In my case, selling with negative equity prevented me from getting back on to the housing ladder for some time, and it is possible that this will be the future facing many.

The challenges faced in renting and in buying mean that for a chunk of the millennial generation, a prolonged period of living with parents can be expected. Around one in four are living at home with parents and reports suggest that within a decade or so this could easily reach one in two. This isn't due purely to housing, but those who I have spoken to suggest that it is the primary reason for living with their parents. While the benefits for millennials living at home include being able to reduce their outgoings and begin the long process of saving, the arrangement often leads to friction between parents and their children.

Imagine this. You have always thought that your son or daughter was likely to need a home and support from you until the age of 16, 18 or 21, and then you suddenly find that your twentysomething or thirtysomething child is back and needing to share your life and personal space once more, for a period that could be indefinite. If that doesn't sound ideal to you, this is often the difficulty facing our parents, who want to do the right thing and help us to get on, but have to change their life and environment once more to accommodate someone who they had hoped would have flown the nest. However, this is the most viable option in the current climate and, in the absence of any financial 'leg up', should be seen as the contribution that a parent makes to helping their millennial child build the necessary credit and savings to help make the move into a place they can call their own.

Essentially, I am proposing the following policies to alleviate the pressure of the housing crisis:

- A mechanism to prevent land banking and other unethical practices

- A mixed economy of housing, particularly through innovations such as decent social housing (paid for by allowing borrowing to fund investment)

- A review of Help to Buy schemes to ensure that service charges are kept reasonable, that mortgage lenders remain wary of applications with only a 5% deposit and that Help to Buy is available in places where house prices are higher, such as (inner) London

- An expansion of the lifetime Isa (Lisa), which is designed to help people save for their first home or for a later-in-life need, and a review to consider higher caps on the amounts that can be invested and reducing the withdrawal fee (currently 25% unless the withdrawal is for one of a handful of very specific reasons). The cap and the withdrawal fee discourage people from seeing the Lisa as an appropriate savings programme.

Alongside these, it is important that we all have an honest conversation about what property is primarily for – where it is seen as a home that provides warmth, shelter and security, and enables people to open a bank account, hold down a regular job and start a family. Society has a stake in ensuring that millennials get the opportunity to rent as early as possible, and move to ownership at a time that suits them. While we continue to view property primarily as an asset, there is no incentive for us as a society to view the housing crisis as a shared problem requiring a shared solution, which it fundamentally is.

MillenniALL

CHAPTER FIVE:

LEARNING AND EARNING IS NOT A LINEAR PROCESS

The days of factory style education are over. A traditional schooling approach that was arguably designed to reinforce class, producing workers at one end and graduates at the other, has begun the irrevocable and inevitable process of disintegration. We are now in a period where information can be accessed readily and does not require much more than a quick search in Google to retrieve. Education as the imparting of knowledge from teacher to student is less relevant and the role of a teacher now is to help a student navigate the cornucopia of online and offline information and differentiate fact from opinion. We are entering an age of ideas, a period where the comfortable consensus in thought has been torn asunder in favour of more radical ideas from the left and the right; this means that the critical thinking skills needed to understand and form well-considered and reasoned opinions are vital.

New ways of learning, new ways of teaching and a focus on the skills necessary to capitalise on the opportunities of the future are driving many millennials to reject the old ways of learning and leading many employers to embrace new ways of developing and training their staff. Traineeships, apprenticeships, internships, moment-of-need learning, degree apprenticeships, flexible learning, intensive learning, online learning, coaching and mentoring, virtual and artificial intelligence-driven learning are all emerging as ways to teach and learn. Many of these methods enable millennials to gain a valuable and relevant education, the experience necessary to demonstrate competence and potential, and the capacity to earn more quickly than through traditional routes.

I don't want to downplay the value of higher education. Undertaking academic study is valuable, empowering and can lead to opportunities and experiences that simply entering the world of work cannot replicate. However, seeing university as the expected avenue for most 18-year-olds is clearly becoming a thing of the past. The most innovative higher education institutions (HEIs) recognise this and are crafting provision that can be accessed at any stage in a person's life. Such flexibility will enable people to learn at a time and a pace that will suit them, ensuring that provision is more student-centred and demand-led, rather than supply-oriented, as currently encouraged by a surfeit of 18-year-olds being chucked in their direction each summer .

However, the problems go back further than that. We talk about millennials being an entrepreneurial generation (which the research does not currently support) and we speak of them increasingly having to pursue self-employment as an option, given the rise of project working and the gig economy, yet our schools are woefully lacking in entrepreneurship education.

GCSEs, A-levels and BTECs in Business talk about the theory of business and may help students to understand some basic principles, but they lack the content that encourages students to get out there and create their first enterprise. Too often, business is seen as a secondary subject at school, an option for those deemed less academic or able. This ignores the fact that the skills that make a good entrepreneur (or at least one with a greater chance of success) are the skills we need in our workforces of the future.

Entrepreneurship is based on creativity, problem-solving, passion, planning, discipline and a willingness to commit and continually develop: these are exactly the skills that employers see as vital in the coming decades. Good entrepreneurship education in schools and colleges goes hand in hand with other aspects of the curriculum and should not be undertaken only by those who are unable to undertake traditional subjects.

While a call to improve entrepreneurship education in schools may seem like an odd subject to include in a book about millennials, since most have left school already, the consequences of a lack of entrepreneurship education runs through all ages and could well be part of the reason why fewer millennials than those from previous generations are starting businesses. A preference for the attainment of degrees has created a generation of people who may hold a degree but find that it does not provide them with the necessary skills required to work in business or start a business. Few post-school or university programmes exist for people who have an entrepreneurial flair, and those that do are often focused on marginalised groups or a specific age range.

The Prince's Trust, for example, does excellent work in encouraging young people into education, training or employment and has some valuable entrepreneurship programmes, but these are aimed at people aged 11–30, which ignores those early stage millennials and xennials who are also in need of support and entrepreneurship education.

The demise of government-backed programmes such as Business Link has left support for entrepreneurs in the hands of local authorities, charities and some banks, whose support and education can be patchy. To realise the potential of all millennials, a renewed commitment to lifelong learning (with entrepreneurship education as a fundamental part of the offer) would go some way to giving millennials the skills and motivation to set up their own business. Leaving it to chance and allowing people to muddle through is no solution and is part of the reason for such a high failure rate in businesses in the UK.

Over the last decade, there has been an explosion in the number of people undertaking apprenticeships, programmes that combine knowledge and skill acquisition with paid employment: the true definition of 'learn and earn'. Apprentices receive training and assessment in the role they have been employed to undertake and have a contract of employment and pay like any other member of staff. From day one, they are an employee with rights, responsibilities and a training programme designed to make them effective and unlock their potential for progression.

Apprenticeships have a long history, dating back to the middle ages, when they lasted several years and enabled successful apprentices to qualify and practice their trade. The introduction of modern apprenticeships in roles such as customer service, retail, digital marketing and management demonstrates that there are few, if any, careers for which an apprenticeship over the right duration and with the right educational content is not an appropriate training vehicle. There have been concerns about the quality of apprenticeship programmes, arguments that some careers are not suitable for apprenticeships and complaints about providers delivering poor quality; however, apprenticeships are increasingly seen as a preferred option for millennials, and their popularity remains undimmed.

An apprenticeship programme has a number of advantages:

1. **You can join the employer of your choice earlier rather than later**

Increasing numbers of employers are entering the apprenticeship market by offering meaningful programmes with good starting wages and the opportunity to progress. No longer is it necessary to wait until after university to apply on the milk round to one of those dream employers – companies such as Rolls Royce, ITV and the big four accountancy practices all have apprenticeship programmes open to those wanting to move straight from school into the workplace.

The introduction of the apprenticeship levy is likely to lead to many larger firms changing the focus of their recruitment from graduates to apprentices. Businesses with a pay bill of more than £3m a year must pay a levy calculated as 0.5% of their payroll, which is available to spend on apprenticeship training and assessment but lost if not spent. This has led to an increase in the number of consultants offering to adjust training programmes to ensure that they can be aligned to an apprenticeship and therefore be eligible for drawdown from the employer's levy account.

While the scheme is in its infancy at the time of writing this book, it has the potential to increase the total number of apprenticeship places available for millennials, with some significant employers potentially offering exciting and well-remunerated programmes. Early indications suggest, however, that the introduction of the levy has dampened apprenticeship starts and will need some work to ensure that it is the right solution for employers and apprentices alike and isn't seen simply as another tax on businesses.

2. You can start earning from day one

Undertaking an apprenticeship makes you an employee with rights, including the right to be paid. Whether it is an apprenticeship in a local employer paying the national apprenticeship wage, or a larger firm paying a full salary of anywhere around the £14,000-£20,000 mark, you can study, acquire skills and add a valuable employer to your CV, while earning a decent salary. By the time graduate peers enter the workplace, they will not have had the experience that you have gained.

3. You can acquire qualifications and achieve a higher education qualification without needing to sacrifice and incur debt

Apprenticeship programmes, particularly the newer apprenticeship standards, have been created by employers, for employers. As a result, the content and qualifications align with the skills and knowledge necessary to be successful in a given role. Many careers now have apprenticeship programmes that go beyond level 3 (A-level equivalent) and some progress up to level 7 (postgraduate equivalent).

While current thinking is that tuition fees for many courses are too high and that reforms to higher education funding have not led to the market-based pricing originally intended, the debt burden for many millennials is increasing. If people can be convinced that an apprenticeship is well-paid, of high quality and enables progression to higher education, particularly through degree apprenticeships, it is very likely that many millennials will choose to undertake this route. Furthermore, apprenticeships do not have an age cap, so many who might have otherwise considered going back to university as mature students may look for apprenticeship opportunities instead.

Do not think that the university sector has taken the shift to apprenticeships lying down. In fact, many universities are aligning themselves to the apprenticeship programme by helping to create and craft degree apprenticeships. These programmes have the advantage of combining the best workplace training and development with a recognised degree and although new, these are likely to be of interest to millennials who still want to study and attain a higher education qualification without the considerable cost.

When I first started out, I was a lecturer in history and sociology at a local further education college teaching GCSEs, A-levels and access to higher education courses. I also acted as a personal tutor and spent much of my time preparing students for their university applications and interviews. All conversations in class revolved around what grades and module results were necessary to get into a particular university; no absence was permitted, unless it was to go to a university open day; and all extracurricular programmes and activities were geared towards bolstering applications and ensuring that students could talk about something other than the subjects they had studied at their interview or in their personal statements. It was expected that everyone (where their grades were acceptable) would go to university, even where the course had very low entry requirements.

Few students spoke of 'employability' and certainly didn't judge the ability of a degree to open doors in industry to be important. An assumption was allowed to permeate through our schools and colleges that possessing a degree would lead to better job prospects and higher earning capacity. Many millennials faithfully trusted this assumption and went to university, and still do, in the belief that good employment opportunities will be waiting at the end.

To my shame, I was a small part of a system that measured success on the progression of students to higher education, and our focus was on ensuring that as many students went to university as possible, irrespective of the quality of the programme or the relevance of the course.

Now I advise late-stage millennials very simply and directly, "If your chosen career does not require a specific degree to be studied for and awarded, and if you cannot justify going to university and incurring significant levels of debt just to live the 'uni life', then think again."

While I undertook HE study and do not regret it – in fact I hold a bachelor's degree, two postgraduate certificates and a master's degree, such is my love of higher education – I would advise people to actively consider an apprenticeship programme as a valuable way of gaining relevant technical skills, acquiring essential experience, developing useful interpersonal and creative skills, and earning a respectable wage.

The nature of learning is also changing and requires those responsible for training delivery to re-examine those solid, dependable but out of date training methods and materials, and freshen them for a new generation. Shorter attention spans and a need for more diversity in activity means that learning should be shorter, sharper, research-focused (allowing things to be Googled, for example) and group-based.

Millennials need to understand the rationale behind or purpose of something and a 'because I said so' statement will not wash; they need to be shown why this learning is relevant to them and how it will fit into their lives and career aspirations. They also expect training to be delivered in a relaxed way, the hierarchical nature of teaching two decades ago has been replaced by a system whereby the trainer is focused on helping them learn in a less pressured, less right-versus-wrong and less win-versus-lose way. The design of learning in the workplace and in our education institutions should reflect the fact that the old authoritarian, chalkboard-style delivery is not what will get the most out of learners today and is likely to cause a negative reaction. No interaction, no challenge, no rationale, no rapport – these are the fastest ways to disengage a millennial learner.

MillenniALL

CHAPTER SIX:

EMPLOYMENT ISN'T ABOUT A JOB FOR LIFE

We know that by 2050 millennials will make up over half of the global workforce, but what will the world of work look like for them?

For previous generations, a career was settled and stable, and many were able to work for one employer for their entire working life. Many pensioners who had worked for 30 years or more had secure pensions – unless they had worked for one of the industries that closed down in the UK and had been made redundant with limited access to a pension, or if they had worked for a business with an unsustainable pension deficit. Final salary pensions were more common, but have increasingly become a thing of the past, replaced by career average pension schemes for some, and meagre stakeholder pensions for others.

If I had worked in industry 20 or 30 years ago, I could have expected to be employed in my role through the ups and downs of production, without anyone asking me whether I would be prepared to work on a zero hours basis. If I'd had a problem, I would probably have been able to consult a union, and providing I was performing to an acceptable level, would probably have retained my work.

Because of structural and economic reforms, there were some mass redundancies. While being made redundant would have been painful, I would have been supported by the welfare state and retrained where possible for the new jobs emerging as a result of creative disruption. It is unlikely that any unemployment benefits would have been means-tested and they would not have been based on a contributory principle.

My skills would have been universal, not subject to changing trends and pressures to continually learn, and formalised education and qualifications would have been considered the primary source of workforce training and development. I would probably have worked in a bureaucratic structure that stressed tenure of service and experience over potential, where I would have needed to know my place and follow a fixed set of protocols around how to achieve my role, getting respite only occasionally when invited on to a project of fixed duration. Job descriptions, job titles and executive perks would have been indicators of progress and aspirational targets.

The workplace that millennials have entered is changing. Yes, there are still mammoth organisations being operated with a command and control structure, with delineation, discipline and tenure positioned above all else, but these have been gradually replaced by organisations that are more nimble, agile and responsive to the needs of millennial workers and customers alike.

When people consider employing millennials, the age-old refrain, "No point employing them, they won't be around for the long term," can often be heard by the reliable pessimist (who conveniently calls themselves a 'realist' – since when has being negative equated with truth and realism? But that's not a conversation for this book!).

It is true that millennials are unlikely to stay with one employer for 20 or 30 years. Research suggests that an average millennial is likely to have 10 different jobs in their working lifetime, which would lead to an average tenure of approximately four-and-a-half to five years per role (assuming a 45 to 50-year working life, which is looking increasingly likely). Many millennials are recognising that due to the changing nature of work, they are likely to have short-term, project-based work, often on a call-on, call-off basis: referred to as the 'gig economy'. Such labour mobility is the new norm and therefore we should begin to see work through three clear lenses:

1. **Work as learning**

2. **Work as enriching**

3. **Work as integration**

1. Work as learning

As work now comprises a series of employment opportunities, it makes sense for millennials to review job opportunities critically to ascertain whether they are likely to be able to learn enough to carry them forward to the next opportunity. When people know that they are unlikely to remain with the same employer for a long time, they prioritise what they can gain from the experience. Earning is linked to learning: those who study more, undertake new roles, gain new skills and experiences and work in multidisciplinary projects are more likely to progress to better-remunerated roles with the same employer or somewhere new. Employers who are awake to this fact and create learning environments that stretch and challenge millennials are more likely to recruit and retain this generation than employers who don't.

Research shows that millennials are among the most entrepreneurial of all the generations, but conversely many of them do not start their own business until their late 30s or 40s, if at all. In one of my recent interviews, Brad Sugars (founder and chair of ActionCOACH) laid it out simply: millennials who want to start a business should look for opportunities to work for others in roles that enable them to learn a range of tasks, for example, sales, operations, marketing and finance. They should seek roles in small businesses, which are more likely to enable exposure to a range of opportunities and challenges. Many entrepreneurial millennials can be of real value to employers who embrace their go-getting qualities and seek to utilise them as 'intrapreneurs'.

Hang on – what?

Intrapreneurs. This isn't some sort of mangled word that I have created while tapping away at my keyboard; this is a description of those who deploy entrepreneurial skills in an organisation that they do not own, usually a corporate of some description. Many millennials want to be able to have a corporate employer on their CV at some point, and those that enable them to bring their intrapreneurial attributes into significant projects are likely to attract the best talent. Those corporates whose culture does not value creativity, ambition a willingness to speak up and speak out, and the ability to learn and make mistakes and take risks are the ones that will not be able to capture the best in the market.

Here's some advice for employers: accept that many of your millennial staff may not hang around with you forever. Don't get too hung up by the fact that they are going to want to try and learn and contribute every day they are in your employment, and that when they feel that the learning has gone, they are either going to pester you for a sideways or upwards move, or are going to search around for the next opportunity. Think of it this way – do you really want someone sitting on your payroll years after they have lost motivation and passion for you and your role? Accept that you are getting the best years from them and that, providing you create an environment that can stimulate them, you are likely to have their loyalty for as long as it is good for both of you.

Here's some advice for millennials: look for opportunities where you can acquire a breadth of experience. Significantly lucrative work will be the result of hard work, patience and endeavour and will come to those who push their own capabilities and perceptions of what can be done, and to those who are prepared to put learning before earning. The world of the big blue chip may be appealing, but don't forget that many small and medium enterprises are exciting, risky and adrenaline-fuelled: an ideal arena in which to cut your teeth and develop your abilities.

2. Work as enriching

For many millennials, the work they undertake and the activities that they enjoy should have a greater purpose: experience trumps possession nowadays. While many will claim that millennials are all 'me, me, me', this could not be further from the truth, as they become a switched-on generation, engaging with civic institutions and promoting social causes. Some commentators try to cite lower participation in voting as evidence that millennials do not care, but that is fundamentally flawed: this generation cares. They care enough to want employment opportunities with organisations that they believe can make a difference, often foregoing more lucrative jobs in the process. When a labour market is as fragmented and insecure as it is now, millennials are looking for more than simply a pay cheque – fulfilment is now a critical factor. As one coaching client of mine once said, "If I'm not going to get the pay, then I want to at least enjoy the job."

Where organisations have a strong vision, mission and values statement that can be seen to permeate throughout all levels, from recruitment practices and staff development through to support and decision-making, there is likely to be greater alignment and loyalty from employees, including millennials. A sense of purpose needs to be communicated regularly, and leaders and managers need to ensure that millennial employees understand their role in making things happen, particularly where the outcomes are more social and civic in nature. Companies that commit to standards and are seen to live and breathe their values are places where millennials are more attracted to work. Sir Richard Branson is quoted as saying that he wrote his books primarily as manuals or handbooks for his staff to help communicate the values that he wanted Virgin companies to be known for; these bestsellers are still embraced and adopted by Virgin employees across the globe.

Here's some more advice for employers: don't be afraid to be clear about the wider ambitions you have for your organisation. Your vision, mission and values (VMV) should not be statements that are simply inserted into the annual report or produced only on request; they should be living, breathing statements that help to tell the world your WHY, your very reason for being. If you don't think you have them, go back and ask yourself why you get up every morning for this company; the positive, juicy stuff that comes from that will form the basis of your VMV. It is a higher purpose, and the enriching nature of doing a great job that can make a real difference, that will help swing a millennial your way.

Also, if you ask yourself why you get up every morning for your company and you cannot say, maybe you need to worry less about the millennials and think more about your own career options.

Here's some more advice for millennials: continue to ask employers to give you their WHY and continue to expect them to respond. If you don't like the answer, continue to search for companies and opportunities that do float your boat. If you get into an organisation and find that the VMV isn't as powerful for you as it seemed to be when you joined, don't be afraid to push back and make it clear that fulfilment and enrichment is critical for you. Look for chances to move to a team or project doing stuff that you would find rewarding, and if the company you work for cannot provide that, don't be afraid to cast your net further. It is frustrating for all concerned when a millennial leaves an organisation after only a matter of months or years, but it is more frustrating for all when a millennial remains, unhappy and disengaged.

3. Work as integration

Everyone loves a bit of work-life balance, don't they? Or is it all about working to live? Maybe I am wrong and it is work hard, play hard?

Or maybe for a millennial, that's all a load of nonsense.

Society has allowed a dichotomy between work and life to emerge, forcing people to see themselves as being somewhere on a continuum between those who submit their whole being to work, and those who simply see work as a way of earning money to do other things. People who make sacrifices for work are held up as ambitious business superstars or loveless robots, depending on who is commenting. People who don't want to progress in their job and are happy to simply fulfil a task and go home are viewed as having a life and being rounded, satisfied individuals or lazy, unambitious jobsworths.

In the era of factories and mass production, people did their work and went home to their families. Work ended at the factory gate on a Friday afternoon and resumed on a Monday morning; the weekend was a time for friends, family and rest. Without emails, the internet or mobile phones, people could not be contacted easily and this ensured that work ended with the punching of the card in the machine (metaphorically and literally).

As communication became more mobile and the world wide web started to be deployed by businesses, work-life balance issues began to dominate. If someone can be contacted by mobile phone or email 24 hours per day, have they ever 'punched their card' and left for the day? It is not uncommon to sit on a Spanish beach and see people flicking through their work mobiles, or holding a conference call, or waving goodbye to their families who are off sightseeing as they stay behind to finish a proposal or document in the warmth of the Mediterranean sun.

When does this become a problem? At what point does it become a howl of complaint, a resentful activity done by someone who feels they have little choice?

Exactly when it is no longer a CHOICE.

A work-life debate emerges when people are working crazy hours in a vain attempt to secure a deal, push a proposal through or ensure that they are not considered a 'slacker'. This is when it is unhealthy, because it is being done for political reasons, or to try to protect a vulnerable position. It isn't being done because of true choice, or because of a passion to learn or enrich, but because of a feeling that if it isn't done, it might weaken their position on their return.

Millennials view work and life in a very different way; instead of conversations about work versus life, they prefer to view it as *work-life integration*. Millennials are comfortable with living in a truly globalised world; the nature of globalisation makes it feel as though the world has contracted and time can be used more flexibly. No longer does the world view business in terms of 08.00–17.00 in their local time zone. If someone wants to work later in the day because their Skype call with a client needs to take place at midnight, then so be it. Organisations no longer have to wait for a fax or telex to be received the following working day (if you are reading this and do not know what either of those are, ask a friend).

Bank holidays, once days when workplaces across the country would shut down, are becoming less relevant as people choose to work and can continue their businesses online without any restrictions on working hours. Do weekends even matter now? Once, a weekend was sacrosanct to many, requiring significant overtime payment or time off in lieu to encourage people to work. Now it is common for people to work on a Saturday and not on a Monday, or to work six, seven or eight consecutive days and then have four or five days off. Nothing is set in stone, and this suits a millennial.

Here comes the advice for the employers: think about how you can construct a physical and virtual environment that encourages millennial staff to integrate their life and working patterns better.

Do you really need them to arrive by 08.30 and not leave until 17.30 with tea breaks and a lunch break dotted in between?

Does the nature of your business REALLY mean that this is the only working pattern available?

Is your office designed in a way that allows your staff to relax and have short interludes where they switch off?

One company I work with has a corner of their office set up for table tennis and pool, where staff can take a short break from the pressure of work. They argue that as well as providing a mental break, this encourages collaboration and idea-generation as staff interact with each other and discuss issues over the pool or ping-pong table. While this shouldn't be seen as a panacea, it does reflect the nature of many smaller, creative businesses where employees weave their life and work together – less work-life balance, and more work-life integration.

Shared working spaces such as WeWork are increasingly becoming more popular than the old-fashioned office companies of the 1990s and 2000s, which demonstrates that people want to work in an environment that is more stimulating and allows them to operate and interact without the constraints of a traditional nine-to-five approach.

Also, consider how your terms and conditions can best suit a millennial. Netflix and Virgin led the way in establishing 'unlimited leave', which allows employees to take time off at short notice for as long or short as necessary. Obviously, there are the usual caveats such as taking time off only if the person is comfortable that they are up to date with their work and that their absence wouldn't unduly affect the work of others, but the message that such a policy statement sends is more important than the statement itself. It is designed to show employees that they are in charge of their working patterns, that they are trusted to make the right decisions for themselves and their business, and that the outcome of work is more important than the level of input.

Remember, talent is attracted to talent. Creating an environment that is appealing for a millennial does not have to cost the earth: take some time to set out your vision, mission and values (VMV), and communicate them across all levels; review the design of your office and your working practices – do they align with the VMV you speak about? How do you sell your business to potential staff who are millennials? Stop thinking that they should be grateful for a job with you, and start to think about how to attract the best talent through selling what you have to offer. Consistency of policy and approach are key: you don't need grand gestures; just be honest, enthusiastic and supportive.

If you are a millennial, look for an employer who allows you to express yourself fully and in a way that meets your aspirations and wishes. Recognise, however, that not every business can provide a 'Virgin-style' menu of terms and conditions, and you will need to compromise a bit. While it is important that a prospective employer can show you their vision and effectively sell their business to you, you can't expect to list a whole host of demands. Both parties are taking a risk – you by committing your time, effort and expertise on the business, them by committing to employ you and give you a chance to develop your career or pursue a passion.

Don't be put off by employers who haven't quite got the whole work-life integration thing; focus on whether they have a commitment to do so and are trying to develop or are open to trying new things. Also, look around the business: are there other millennials? Do they seem to like working there? Engage with them on LinkedIn and see whether they enjoy working for the company. Find out as much as you can before you list your demands.

Finally, don't mislead. Don't pretend you will be there for the long haul if you know that you won't. Integrity is critical. If you want to use this opportunity to progress your skills and experience, be honest about this; tell them in a positive and friendly way. If they don't like that answer, they won't offer you the role and you will find another that is more suitable for your own dreams and goals.

What else can millennials do to get the type of work that they want, without having to take permanent, full-time employment? Don't underestimate the value of the gig economy. While it may have received a bad press recently, with the media, politicians and unions all highlighting the lack of stability and employment rights associated with such working arrangements, the benefits to a millennial can be significant. For the many millennials who wish to experience rather than possess, to access rather than own, the ability to pick and choose what assignments to work on – with some say over selection based on project outcomes, the vision of the contracting 'employer' and the financial remuneration – can be attractive. This route has much to offer an individual who may want to travel around, try different projects and build up a range of experience and references that would enhance any LinkedIn profile.

There is an increasing trend towards that of the 'digital nomad'. While the ability for people to travel to far-flung locations and continue to work is not new, it is becoming far more common, thanks to technological advances and the desires of many millennials to combine travel and gig working. Several countries are now encouraging this and introducing the necessary legal structures. Estonia, for example, has introduced an e-residency scheme that will enable location-independent people to live and work in Estonia relatively easily. While countries continue to welcome more millennials who wish to combine work and travel, the rise in the numbers of people electing to be digital nomads will continue apace.

MillenniALL

CHAPTER SEVEN:

RELATIONSHIPS ARE BLURRY, MESSY AND LATE

Debt, lack of stable employment, the inability to own a property and other structural challenges face the millennial generation. No other postwar generation has experienced such a challenging environment in which to grow up, start a career or build a business. It isn't any wonder that relationships are also suffering: millennials are later to start a relationship, later to marry, and later to start a family, also having smaller families when they finally do. This doesn't mean, however, that millennials aren't interested in relationships and other people, just that they may choose to defer the C-word: *commitment*.

Millennials are also the first generation to openly begin to challenge the traditional definitions and labels of sexuality, being more comfortable with the plurality and fluidity that truly underpins sexuality. Furthermore, contrary to what people assume, the millennial generation seems to be turning its back on being sexually active, with many not undertaking significant sexual activity.

What could be causing such a shift in sexual behaviour and relationship-formation? The first is apparent: more millennials are living longer at home with their parents. If you ever wanted to see your sex drive plunge to new lows, try to engage in sexual activity with a partner knowing your parents are a matter of inches away from your bedroom. While the idea of sneakily indulging while your parents aren't at home is exciting and novel for a teenager, it doesn't quite have the same feel for a twentysomething. Awkward questions, accidental encounters in the morning and not being able to do a walk of shame quietly due to wandering past your lover's parents and children all sitting around the breakfast table adds to a sense that this is not a place to re-enact the scenes from *Fifty Shades of Grey*.

Second, millennials are becoming more nuanced about what they consider to be 'sex'. When asked whether they have had sex 'recently' they are more likely to say no, viewing sex as intercourse, and other forms of sexual activity as less significant. Improved sex education in schools has also led to a revision of sex and sexual activity, and the levels of teenage pregnancy are lower for millennials than for other generations at that age.

Millennials are also focusing on other activities that give them satisfaction, such as travel, work and civic activities; they are seeking to enjoy wider experiences, and this means that the satisfaction they could get from an immediate physical relationship is less important. Where a physical urge needs to be satisfied, the ease with which someone can now find no-strings attachments, or the thrill of regular dating with different people, is personified in the multiplicity of online dating applications and websites, ranging from long-standing and established sites such as match.com through to 'easy-swipe' apps like Tinder or Grindr.

As I mentioned before, I am on the cusp of the millennial generation, having been born in the 1980s, and I spoke about people born in the late 1970s and early 1980s as being more accurately referred to as 'xennials' or 'early stage millennials'.

Early stagers like me entered the world of dating and relationships in a mostly analogue age, where meeting someone would entail a trip out one evening that would be structured like this: our group would meet in a local pub and take advantage of the cheap drinks offers as well as something to eat if we had entered the pub early enough (which was often the case if we had met to watch Saturday afternoon or early evening football on the pub's TV screen); we would then progress to a bar that played music, where we would be packed like sardines, and we would begin the process of chatting to people we found attractive (or as attractive as we could judge based on our increasingly poor visibility, affectionately referred to as 'beer goggles'). The bar acted as the warm-up to the local nightclub, where we would queue outside to enter, chatting to more people about the queue, the bouncers and so on.

Eventually we would enter the nightclub and continue to drink, dance and enjoy the company of those we were attracted to, which often was more about who found us attractive or interesting. On some occasions, things would progress, and on other nights things wouldn't; either way, we would all get a taxi home and spend the next day nursing our hangovers. If we had been successful that evening, we would spend the next day potentially texting someone to see if they wanted to go out some time, and so the dating process would begin (assuming they responded favourably).

Looking back on those times, that seems to have been a hell of a lot of work! That strategy was time-consuming and costly, with a very hit-and-miss conversion rate. If that didn't work, people had to take out lonely heart ads in the local paper, and hope that someone would decode the letters (GSOH anybody?), that they could be bothered to write a letter in response and walk to the postbox. Swiping is so much easier!

The advent of online dating was helpful for the busy early stager who could now chat to people, find out more and arrange a date without having to leave the comfort of their home. If you didn't like someone, you could ignore them or block them, without ever having to remember the night before. If you did like someone, you could discover more about their interests, hobbies and passions before going on a date – it was almost nigh on impossible to do this on a night out with all the noise, lights and heavy alcohol consumption. Online dating was originally expensive, with memberships and subscriptions being the expected business model. Few free dating platforms existed; those that did were not necessarily the ideal places to find a romance.

Apps such as Tinder are online dating 2.0, the natural result of technology enabling frictionless interaction. Since time began, people have enjoyed the thrill of the chase and the ability to flirt, find out about other people and find attraction in others. Current technologies can provide all the fun without the friction for millennials who are short of time and lack the desire to commit too much to the process of dating. Whether you swipe left or swipe right, you are in control and can engage with a range of people on a 24/7 basis for anything from a heavy romance to a simple hook-up: most preferences and interests are available for those looking.

Increasingly, we see more people declaring that their relationship started as a result of online or mobile dating, and this should not necessarily be seen as a bad thing.

Those who are concerned about online or mobile dating talk about the inherent risk in meeting someone that they haven't physically met before. It is certainly true that we can get only a certain amount of information from a profile on a site, but is that any less safe than the person we meet in the noisy, dark, alcohol-fuelled surrounds of a nightclub? Millennials need to be aware of the risks of arranging to meet someone with whom they have had online contact only, just in the same way that we used to warn people about where and how they would meet someone with whom they had barely had contact, but had encountered at a bar or club. The fact is that there are good people in the world and not-so-good people. The not-so-good people will use all avenues to take advantage, and the good people will use all avenues to try to create genuine connections.

Technology is enhancing, not replacing, interpersonal and other social interactions. Apps still require you to meet the person if you wish to date or hook up. There is no app yet that can fully replicate the human and physical nature of dating and sex, so people still need to commit the time and physical presence needed: an app simply speeds this process up and helps to filter out the people unlikely to be of interest. With the advent of new robotics and artificial intelligence, however, it is possible that a whole new industry of romance could emerge, allowing people to engage in intimate and physical relationships with machines, although whether this can truly replicate human interaction remains to be seen.

Sexuality is less defined and binary for millennials, with experimentation and a refusal to conform to straight or gay labels becoming more prevalent. Recent research suggested, for example, that 50% of British millennials consider themselves bisexual, compared with around 23% of the general British population. Research carried out using the Kinsey scale – a scale of 0 (exclusively heterosexual) to 6 (exclusively homosexual) also indicates that more millennials are scoring themselves somewhere along the scale and anecdotal information suggests that millennials are less hung-up by strict definitions of their sexuality, viewing it as a shifting continuum rather than a binary choice.

"With each generation, people see their sexuality as less fixed in stone," the polling organisation YouGov reports.

New definitions have emerged that are being used by the millennial generation to explain and encompass the range of different options available, including the following:

'Solosexual' refers to those who prefer to masturbate, sometimes on camera to others, sometimes alone, and prefer this to dating and a physical relationship with others.

'Sapiosexuals' are those who value intelligence over any other qualities, irrespective of the individual's sex.

'Demisexuals' are individuals who struggle to enter a physical relationship with anyone until they have a strong romantic connection, again irrespective of the individual's sex.

To add to this, there are terms such as 'pansexual' and 'heteroflexibility', all increasingly common in millennial conversations around sexuality.

What all these definitions have in common is an underlying recognition that states of sexuality are not as fixed as previous generations would have you think. It is possible to be on a continuum and also to have different preferences. As the millennial pop sensation Miley Cyrus once declared, "I am literally open to every single thing that is consenting and doesn't involve an animal, and everyone is of age … I'm down with any adult … who is down to love me."

Personal conversations I have had with millennials on this subject indicate that an increasingly open and inclusive society has made many feel more comfortable about admitting to being less dogmatic in their sexuality; furthermore, as millennials are now increasingly experience-driven, they are more interested in deep connections with people, irrespective of their sex or gender.

It is therefore not surprising that the millennial generation is also more supportive of LGBTQ+ rights and overwhelmingly supportive of policies such as the introduction of same-sex marriages.

Alongside this, there is a rise in the plurality of relationships, with more millennials viewing monogamy as less important in more casual relationships, often choosing to retain monogamy for 'the one'. This has had an impact on public policy and business, as lawmakers scrabble to keep up with changing views and find a backlash when a policy is proposed that could be seen as discriminatory, and business leaders burnish their credentials around diversity in the workplace.

This does not mean that there are not still pockets of discrimination or that LGBTQ+ rights have been firmly entrenched in society, but it is clear that members of the millennial generation are far more comfortable with their own identities and the identities of others and are prepared to stand up for equality for all.

The increasingly casual nature of relationships for millennials helps to explain why many choose to defer more serious relationships until a later stage. This does not mean that when millennials enter into a serious relationship that it is fundamentally different in style from those of other generations. In fact, millennials still want to marry and have children, but are leaving this to a time when they are in a position to be able to do so.

It is a fact that we now live in a more sexualised society – the spread of the internet, the downgrading of significance of sexual behaviour and the establishment of open sex education have all contributed to a world where sex is no longer a taboo subject. The creation of Netflix, TV on demand and realistic video games have made a 'watershed' time largely redundant for those in their teenage years and above; this is coupled with the use of coarser language on podcasts, daytime TV and daytime radio dramas – things that wouldn't have been considered acceptable 20 years ago.

It is through this prism that we should now view the world and human connection, rather than harking back to a golden period that never was. The fact that sex and sexuality are subjects that millennials are comfortable with discussing makes for a safer and more open environment – we are in a world of #metoo, where inappropriate behaviours are not simply brushed under a carpet, but challenged and atoned for, where people learn that relationships are based on equality and not a power imbalance.

We live in a time when sexually transmitted diseases are discussed and treated more openly, where HIV and AIDS are not the stigmatic issues they were in the 1980s and 90s, and where the number of teenage pregnancies has reduced due to better and more open sex education. This isn't to say that the world is perfect, and that new challenges and dangers don't exist for millennials and post-millennials – they do – but a more open and tolerant society has more of a chance of tackling new social ills than the closed societies of the past.

MillenniALL

CHAPTER EIGHT:

IT'S OK IF YOU ARE NOT AN OVERNIGHT AMAZING SUCCESS

I've been really keen to get to this chapter as I am moving to the third phase of the book, which is all about imparting some of my personal experience about life as a millennial. Too often there is great pressure for millennials to feel that they ought to have it all and achieve early and quickly. We are constantly bombarded with messages about success as well as videos on Facebook, Instagram and YouTube about how to make it, how to lead better lives, and how to be more healthy, wealthy and wise. If we watched every video and read every article, post or blog about how to be successful, we would never have any time left to go and BE successful.

I have researched many influencers and 'experts' on Instagram and I'd estimate that approximately 80% of their accounts are mostly pushing some form of improvement programme or are populated with images designed to promote the benefits of success and #hustle – cars, champagne, expensive holidays and photos with good-looking people in sunny locations.

Every day, a glance at my Facebook feed reveals another polished video telling me that if I want to achieve everything, I need to work harder and smarter than everyone else. Each video seems to be a revision of the video posted before – there are few original pieces of advice. The trick is to take one, use a few different words, edit it to a high standard and push it out.

Don't get me wrong. There is nothing wrong with any of this – for some it is inspiring and motivational, a valuable and timely reminder that success doesn't fall from the sky, that it takes hard work and commitment. However, very few accounts ever show the darker, tougher side of aspiration and #hustle. We do not see the personal cost to many; we do not understand their challenges; and are not let in on the difficulties that they encounter daily.

Be in no doubt, the life of an entrepreneur or leader is not always Moët and Mercedes: it is mostly monotony and melancholy.

Am I doing this right?

Is this what I should be doing?

> Am I cut out for it all?

> Why am I not having the success that Gary Vee has? I listen to his podcasts, watch his videos, attend his events and read his books!

These are the refrains I hear regularly from millennials who have been fed a diet of self-help books and videos. Whether they are seeking to start or grow a business, progress in their career, improve their health and fitness or mental wellbeing, we are increasingly creating a society where 'wisdom' comes from people online telling fables, creating motivational videos set to dramatic music or hosting podcasts or vlogs that are designed to show you how quick and easy it is to be an overnight success. In the drive to hear these 'experts', some millennials have missed the memo that says how tough and time-consuming true improvement can be.

In preparation for this chapter, I decided to browse my Instagram feed for a short while and count and classify the different posts that appeared (sad, I know). I looked at the first 100 that appeared on my feed and made a crude but effective classification. At the end of the process it became clear that over three-quarters of all posts were quotes or advice, product promotion or people taking photos of themselves looking good (generally to promote a product or service or offer advice). Only a quarter of all posts were jokes or memes or general photo sharing of life, relaxation, families and so on (without any advice attached).

Again, I want to stress that having motivational posts and quotes is not bad; offering good, sound advice isn't bad; showing people the progress you have made and the rewards of your hard work and success isn't bad – I myself do this. However, we tend to use social media platforms mostly to show the good, the success, the trinkets, the toys and the lifestyle that is achieved; and we neglect to show the blood, sweat and tears that a journey of personal and professional development truly involves.

Instagram is a perfect example of this – a platform dedicated to photo-sharing has become a prism through which people project the positive and downplay the negative. This runs the risk of giving millennials a false sense of the speed and magnitude of success. We are already aware that millennials by their nature have an innate impatience and a greater desire than previous generations to accelerate their life, and the 24/7 stylised nature of Instagram means that "get rich quick," "get that great body quick," or "get those millions through cryptocurrency," are messages that permeate all the time. Members of generation X had a rather different experience, with only infomercials and newspaper adverts to tell them about such schemes. Prior generations would have needed to be in the same physical location as a speaker or salesperson to hear what strategies they could deploy for success.

Social media has accelerated and amplified the message, meaning that we are surrounded by success and happiness all the time. A whole industry has emerged – that of the 'influencer' – people who are paid to sponsor and promote products and services by using their large following on platforms such as Instagram. These individuals have often gained fame by filming and posting to YouTube; they have a great deal of sway over their followers and can use this for commercial advantage. Many of these influencers charge significant fees for speaking and promotional work based on their media following. Businesses have recognised that user-generated content is one of the best ways to put their products and services in front of millennial prospects, so they harness the power of social media influencers, paying generous sums for such access.

However, what more influencers need to do is to recognise the power of their personal brand and ensure that their audience sees the tougher, darker, more difficult times of their lives. They need to give advice that is honest, straightforward and not promoted by a particular brand, but is based on what they genuinely believe to be true.

Several influencers are actively doing this, people like Dan Osman – a well-known fitness and nutrition coach who gives advice based on real research and evidence and is not tied to a particular concept. He gives an unvarnished view of fitness, health and wellbeing on Facebook and Instagram, helping people to cut through the multiplicity of 'advice' that is out there, some of which is untrue and potentially dangerous. He also shows the difference between how he looked when he was competing for fitness model competitions, and how he looks now – the latter being far healthier than before. Seeing the challenges he had to overcome and the impractical lifestyle he adopted for those competitions helps to give some realism about the world of fitness modelling, against a backdrop of easy insta-stories and posts from others who make it seem a straightforward process. You can follow Dan on Instagram (@ace_dan_osman) to find out more.

For those struggling with a startup business, I'd recommend the *StartUp* podcast hosted by Alex Blumberg and Lisa Chow. While Alex isn't a millennial, he does use his podcast series to highlight the highs and lows of starting up a business, being prepared to share his defeats as well as his victories. For a startup millipreneur it's really important to find resources, podcasts or articles from people who are prepared to talk about the difficulties they have experienced as well as their successes; hearing only from entrepreneurs about how great their businesses are gives a skewed impression of the ease by which a business can be started.

It isn't easy. It takes graft (or as people love to call it #hustle) and will often take someone to the edge of their sanity or bank overdraft, or both. Hearing and reading stories from other entrepreneurs who have struggled, who have made mistakes, who haven't tested and measured their strategies properly or who haven't hired well, are vital lessons for the new business owner and should be shared as widely as possible. Alex's podcast offers a good example of this.

In my interviews for social media platforms, I speak to millennial entrepreneurs who have had success as well as those undergoing the long, slow-burn process of building a business – people like Luke Pitkin, a client of mine and the founder of Sniiper, a software platform that will greatly change the nature of the relationship between company recruiters and recruitment agencies in the future. Luke speaks honestly about his initial desire to set up, his sacrifices to get the business started and the ongoing pleasures and pains of running a technology startup aiming to build enough traction to secure the right level of investment for further business growth. For every millennial who makes it in business quickly, there are many like Luke who play the long game.

I work with millennial entrepreneurs to help them to take their five and six-figure businesses to seven figures and beyond. They routinely overestimate what they can achieve in the short term, and underestimate what they can achieve in the long term. Just because we compound our learning now, or progress through a hierarchy in a company quicker, or get that pizza delivered to our door really quickly, it doesn't mean that our business will become an overnight success.

Since the start of time, whenever there has been the opportunity to earn and accrue wealth, there have been the opportunities for the get-rich-quick schemes. From the Gold Rush in the US, through to Ponzi schemes, fake mediums communicating with the dead for cash, and an attempt to sell off the Eiffel Tower, through to more recent scams such as those of Frank Abagnale and Bernie Madoff, there have always been people promising to make other people wealthy and successful for an initial investment. (To be honest, I'm just pleased that I am currently occupying my time writing this book or I would probably be typing my bank details into an email reply to a Nigerian prince who contacted me recently asking for a loan to help him secure an inheritance that is being denied to him.)

While obviously not the same as these traps, there are schemes and business models being promoted as failproof concepts that can make anyone prepared to invest a significant amount of money. We hear of Amazon drop-ship millionaires and my inbox is full of emails asking me whether I would like to learn the secrets of these individuals (for a small fee, of course). We read of people who have started eBay businesses and are now sitting on small fortunes, and we learn of people making serious amounts of cash from bitcoin.

The latest trend that is proving popular with millennials, particularly those who are keen to enter the world of entrepreneurship, is network marketing, otherwise known as multilevel marketing (MLM). This model has been in existence for many years, and a number of well-known companies operate on an MLM basis.

The principle behind MLM is simple. Independent business owners (IBOs) buy the right to market and sell a range of products in return for a commission from the total sales, which is not necessarily where the major income is made. The IBO finds others who wish to be involved (let's call that individual 'IBO2'), brings them into the opportunity and gets financial recognition based on the sales of IBO2 as well as for their own sales. If IBO2 brings in IBO3, then IBO1 gets financial recognition for their own sales, plus the sales of IBO2 and IBO3.

Sounds simple to set up? That's because it pretty much is. Many people might scoff at those involved in such programmes, but I believe they are a great place to start developing the skills necessary to run a business. The amount of effort that many people I know, some of whom are clients, are putting in to running these businesses is phenomenal; they are gaining their apprenticeship in business on the job: branding, marketing, selling and negotiating, often at high levels of intensity. If you are good at sales and marketing, you can make a decent return for your own sales. If you are good at creating teams of other independent salespeople, that is how you can compound your revenue.

This is not, however, a get-rich-quick scheme. For most people, MLM can provide a useful side income, but not a route to financial freedom or millions in the bank, contrary to what may be posted by those involved on their social media. What MLM can provide a millennial beyond a #sidehustle is the ability to learn key business skills over an extended period. Essentially, the art of business is the ability to sell. As my friend, Alison Edgar, award-winning sales trainer and speaker says, "Without successful selling there is no business." The sales and marketing skills needed to make a decent MLM venture can be transferred into a bigger business in the long run. (Hear Alison's great pearls of sales wisdom by following her on Twitter: @aliedgar13).

Personal and professional progression takes time. Here is a piece of advice for you: take that need to accelerate and apply a gentle brake. Not too much, but enough to recognise that success comes from the consistent deployment of skill, immersion in learning and the application of that learning on a test-and-measure, trial-and-error basis.

Life is a long game – your activity in the world of work and business is likely to span at least four decades (unless you are one of the small percentage that manage to accrue enough wealth to retire early). It is critical that you create a game plan that can take you through a fixed period of time. We know that setting specific goals and having a focus on the long term can help an individual make positive progress towards the life and business they want.

So here is my advice:

1. Planning

• Start with a 10-year plan

This will be a broad plan for what your life will look like in the future, and that is OK at this stage. What is most important is that you have an idea about what that 10-year plan for your life, business or career looks like. Try and be as specific as possible and as aspirational as you want. What experiences do you want to have? What do you want to own or share? What sort of person do you want to become?

• Define a 5-year plan

This plan has a more defined structure than the 10-year plan as you will be able to think more carefully about the next five years. Remember, this is halfway towards your 10-year master plan and so should reflect that.

• Specify your 3-year plan

This plan should be far more specific: three years is not that far away. What are the things you want to have achieved in the next three years as you progress towards your master plan?

• Detail your 1-year plan

Your next year is essential to your chances of success or failure. Brad Sugars once told me that too many people overestimate what they can achieve in the short term and underestimate what they can achieve in the long term.

The rationale for starting with the 10-year plan and moving down to the one-year plan is that with this perspective, you are less likely to cram too much into your one-year plan – if your plan isn't realistic or achievable, you are likely to lose heart and get frustrated. Keep it simple, recognising that it will require you to put more activity in and receive less back at this stage: the compounding effect of actions will come in later years.

- **Create your 90-day plan**

Those who set micro-goals on a quarter-by-quarter basis are more likely to see their actions through, stay the course and fulfil their dreams and goals. Set three key goals for a quarter that can help you achieve your one-year plan; be specific and make sure that you are clear how those goals will help you get one step closer to the bigger plans.

Holding the course can be tough and frustrating, particularly in a fast-paced world where results are needed quickly. Recognise that fulfilling every one of your 90-day goals is an achievement in itself and take the time to reward yourself for getting it done. As you complete more tasks, you will get closer to your one-year plan; as you pass the one-year stage and continue to do 90-day plans, you will get closer to your three-year-plan, and so on. Take the time to build your personal or business brand and be prepared to give detail and attention to the small things.

If you would like to find out more about the templates I use with my clients and how I hold them to account through my online and face-to-face mastermind programmes, drop me or my team a message and we will send you a link to our *Planning Vault*.

2. Build patience and resilience

Remember, building something takes time and patience. If everything were as easy as Instagram suggests, everyone would have a shortcut to success. Not every millennial does.

When people ask me about my favourite book, they are often surprised with the answer they get: *Oh, The Places You'll Go!* by Dr Seuss. Why? It talks about the highs and lows of life and encompasses all the challenges that someone will encounter on their journey of life because:

> I'm sorry to say so but, sadly it's true, that Bang-ups and Hang-ups can happen to you.

We have all had bang-ups and-hang ups and the book reminds us of the most important lesson:

> So be sure when you step. Step with care and great tact and remember that Life's a Great Balancing Act.

Failure will come to you and should be seen as the natural consequence of trying. The very nature of trying means that there may well be failure, as well as the possibility of success, and history is littered with those who have tried and failed and failed numerous times but have managed to bounce back and move on to great success.

Dr Seuss himself was rejected by publishers 27 times before his first book was accepted and published. The rest of his literary success is easily found if you search on Google and I encourage you to take heart from this – he pressed on, confident that his work was worthy of publication and that in time people would recognise this.

Be confident in who you are and what you have to offer the world; rejection is natural and can be expected most times but those who ultimately succeed are those individuals who continue to move forward, listening to feedback, adapting and being relentless in their quest to achieve.

James Buckley-Thorp, founder of the international brand Rupert and Buckley, started his business as a university student with £40 and a hell of a lot of patience. The business is now worth more than £3m and is growing rapidly; however, it took James several years to get to this position. The long game was necessary but worth it for him and his team. You can follow James and his quest to help over half-a-million product and retail startups on Instagram: @jbuckleythorp.

3. Avoid all show and no substance

Do not start a business expecting it to be the next Apple. Don't shout about your business or try to do anything showy. Allow your quality, performance and success to speak for itself.

Show your capability through execution: effective execution is all the world needs to see while you build a successful and commercial business.

Too many people think simply designing a logo, starting a Facebook page and telling the world all about it will be enough. If only this were true. Too many people use their platforms to talk about nothing, waxing lyrical about how their product or service is going to revolutionise the world, even though it has never sold and hasn't even been finished yet. The number of people that I see calling themselves an 'entrepreneur' with simply 'Coming soon...' below an Instagram post of them posing always surprises me. I respect those who graft, the ones who are building their business slowly but surely, who are seeking advice and who are happy to have their successes speak for themselves.

4. Learning from failure

Don't be afraid of failing – it may happen. If it does, learn from your failure and consider how your next business will be different and better.

If you struggled to identify your unique selling point in the first business, get it right for the second. If you didn't identify your cashflow gap and take action to close it in the first, make sure you do it for the second.

In the UK we fear failure more than our friends across the Atlantic do. **False Expectations Appearing Real** – that's what FEAR really is. We allow ourselves to see failure as a cataclysmic event; we put a great deal of store behind failure instead of encouraging people to try again. I challenge you now: go away and think about a successful entrepreneur in this country who has NEVER experienced failure to some degree; I promise you will struggle to give me a name. That's because failure always happens, we experience failure in our businesses regularly, it is the IMPACT that determines whether we survive or not. To negate the impact, we need to accept the failure, learn from it and put in place systems and structures to reduce the likelihood of it happening again.

If you are a millennial considering that startup, think on this: 91% of all small businesses survive their first-year trading, but only 40% of all small businesses survive beyond five years. Failure is a strong possibility. A range of factors can lead to failure – poor cash flow, an inability to sell, weak planning, being overleveraged, focusing time and effort on non-revenue producing activities. These are the lessons I hear from past and current clients and which I, as a business coach, work to help millennial business owners improve. The chances of failure can be reduced through some simple processes, plans and a clear focus on what is essential for your business.

Learn from failure; minimise its impact.

5. Take action

They say that the best time to plant a tree was yesterday, and that the second-best time is today. I believe in a similar approach when it comes to taking action to build a business.

You don't need to wait for a big idea, you don't need to spend time forever creating a brand, a logo, a product or service. Get out there and sell, check that the market is interested in what you have to offer. Sell and worry about the delivery after you know that it is viable. Get started on something that you can do outside your day job. Emma Jones, founder of Enterprise Nation, talks about the "5–9, not the 9–5," and it is a pertinent point: what can you be doing after work to create the commercial and profitable business you desire without sacrificing everything on a whim? How can you get your existing employer to create the right environment for you to become an intrapreneur?

The reality is that not everyone needs to be a business owner to demonstrate entrepreneurial qualities; you should explore whether you would like to be an entrepreneur in an existing business, particularly if you want to learn before you strike out on your own.

6. Get to know people

Network, network, network. Get out and meet people. Get used to talking to a range of people, offering value and explaining what you do. Business doesn't simply come from a Facebook profile, an Instagram account and a landing page: it comes from getting to know, like and trust people. Digital platforms can only accentuate a great reputation, they cannot make one for you from scratch.

Some of the people you meet may become clients, some may have a network of people who want to know, others may simply raise your standards of performance just by being around. There are great Facebook groups you can join to supplement your face-to-face networking and relationship-building, but never do it at the expense of getting out and meeting people.

If you want to dip your toe into the world of Facebook Group Networking, feel free to search for The Millennials Circle and make a request to join. In here, you will be able to share experiences, build relationships and develop your business and personal leadership skills. Never underestimate the importance of talking to people – lots of people, people online and offline, just talk.

7. Stop investing in yourself last

Invest in yourself. You are going to be your business and your brand, so make sure you invest in you. Get a coach or a mentor, join a mastermind group, read widely, attend conferences, go to workshops and training sessions. Seek help and advice. Remember that the best support and advice isn't necessarily given away free, so recognise that you need to invest and consider how you could possibly make the necessary investment to fast-track your learning and development.

Even though I run bootcamps, masterminds, and one-to-one coaching for some of the brightest and best millennial entrepreneurs around, I personally invest significant sums in my own development. I have two coaches currently and am a member of a fantastic mastermind that gives me great ideas, pushes me on, and enables me to grow as a coach, trainer and business owner. Don't undervalue the power of being supported by the right type of people, particularly as you start.

Whether you are running a business or progressing your career in someone else's organisation, don't let failure put you off. Don't let failure shape who you are and the person you will become. Successful people are often failures who have learned, stood up again and tried once more.

MillenniALL

CHAPTER NINE:

FEELING A SENSE OF EXPECTATION AS A MILLENNIAL MALE

hesitated about writing this chapter.

Is it right to have a chapter talking solely to men?

Why does it have to be just for men? Why can't women benefit from the chapter, or have their own chapter?

Having deliberated, I decided to write this chapter, because I felt that I had something to say. Most of the people who contact me for advice and guidance are millennial men.

On occasion, I feel like a priest in the confessional box, listening to the concerns of millennial males seeking to know themselves better in the world in which they inhabit. The world is very different from the one occupied by their fathers, grandfathers and great-grandfathers, and the way in which masculinity is viewed and projected needs to be revised. That's why I've decided to offer some thoughts on this topic in the hope that it will stimulate a wider discussion about the role of the millennial male today.

What does millennial masculinity look like and why is it so different from previous generations? Social norms shift at a glacial pace, but it is important to recognise that they do shift, absolutely. Only a third of millennial males consider themselves 'masculine', compared to double that proportion for baby boomer males. This is partly because the definition of what it is to be a man was very different at the turn of the 20th century from what it was at the turn of the 21st century.

Social norms change with every new generation. Baby boomers experienced a world that included the women's liberation movement, a relaxation in the processes for securing a divorce or an abortion and more latitude for explicit content in literature, all of which heralded changes in what society considered acceptable or otherwise.

Generation X experienced a world of easy money, alternative edgy comedy, the explosion of 18–30 holidays and the rave culture, again shifting the narrative over boundaries of acceptability.

In turn, millennials are also different from previous generations. The number of people going out to clubs has declined, as many nightclub operators will tell you when they close clubs or reduce their footprint. The lad culture that was prevalent in the 1980s and 90s has faded – fewer men are going out and behaving in a way that was commonplace 20 years ago. More men are openly relabelling (or refusing to label) their sexuality. More men believe in equality at home and in the workplace, with many becoming champions for fair pay, fair access and positive action to help establish a balance between men and women. It is not uncommon for men to take a leading role in championing gender equality, LGBTQ+ rights and other causes because of their changing views about what is considered acceptable.

The idea that being masculine is about being heroic, solid and unemotional – otherwise known as being the 'strong, silent type' – is gradually fading away, which explains the fall in the number of millennial males who view themselves as 'masculine'. For these individuals, being masculine is now about something else.

Gone are the days when men occupied the role of sole breadwinner, while their partner (usually a woman) stayed at home bringing up their children, occasionally working to make extra money on the side.

Gone are days when a father was seen as the person who enforced discipline, was scary and unapproachable, and did not share in the caring aspects of parenting.

During my childhood, my father was remote and tough. He believed in a parenting style that he had adopted from his own experience with his father – it was driven by unqualified and unquestioning respect for his position as 'head of the household', a belief in the merits of corporal punishment if he did not get obedience and a belief that domestic responsibilities were not to be shared equally between all. He demonstrated a lack of consideration for any of my emotional needs.

He could not understand why I would not do more 'boy' things, but he also wanted me to push myself hard with my studies, so he could have a successful son.

No vulnerability was present, no self-awareness from him.

It was traditional, passed down throughout the ages, and as hard as stone. Our relationship was not easy, and I vowed that I would never be that sort of father to my own son. I believed that respect was earned, rather than given, that reward and sanction should be merit-based and proportionate, and that the emotional wellbeing of a child was paramount. I am sure that I am not the only millennial male to reflect on his experience of a traditionally masculine father and to resolve not to be like that when it was my turn.

The 'new masculinity' has some distinct features that make it different from previous iterations and I believe that these are three of the key ones:

1. **Vulnerable and self-aware**

2. **Challenging and non-conforming**

3. **Championing and growing**

Vulnerable and self-aware

Millennial males do not believe that strength is projected from being cold, emotionless and without a sense of vulnerability. They recognise that people are comfortable with showing imperfections, admitting mistakes and appreciating that they have flaws as well as perfections.

Millennial masculinity is about understanding what makes us strong and what makes us weak, and that showing the world this takes courage and is a source of strength. Holding to a principle of silence and a reluctance to admit errors, concerns or problems simply stores up trouble — we are human pressure-cookers and if we cannot use our vulnerability to release some of the pressure, we are likely to explode. It is no surprise that mental health is a major concern for males and that many more males than females attempt suicide. As we create a society that is comfortable to talk about what makes us happy, unhappy, concerned and stressed, we give permission for men to be open and honest and such vulnerability helps to reduce the duration and intensity of any mental health issues.

Challenging and non-conforming

Millennial males do not understand why traditional structures and roles must be the way that they have been prescribed by men from previous generations.

> Why wouldn't you want to share in the joys of parenthood and take a more equal role in bringing up a child?

> Why wouldn't you want to do your equal share of running your house?

> Why wouldn't you want to step aside for the other
> partner if they want to be the primary earner and
> you want a more domestic lifestyle?

These are all things that millennial males ask. Many of them will still go out and be the primary earner or have less of a role in bringing up the children, but they want to have the choice. The rise of the new femininity, where women demand the choice to go back to work or to be the primary earner, naturally complements the new masculinity as men increasingly challenge preconceived ideas about their role in society and refuse to conform to traditional labels. The introduction of shared paternity and maternity leave has sent a message to millennial fathers that they can experience child-rearing more if they so wish.

More men are also questioning why everything must be labelled, why everything must be neatly put into a box and why life must follow a certain path. As they challenge the status quo, more men feel comfortable in adopting a persona that feels more authentic for them.

In his book, *The Mask of Masculinity*, Lewis Howes talks about masks that men wear and argues that when men give themselves permission to remove the mask and be their natural selves, they are happier, more fulfilled and more successful. As more millennial men recognise this and challenge the assumptions and norms handed on by previous generations, more of them will throw off their masks and assume more content, authentic roles.

Championing and growing

Millennial men are more likely to believe in the potential of all, irrespective of gender, sexuality or ethnicity, and are more likely to align themselves to campaigns and causes that champion equality. What has been striking about the #MeToo campaign has not just been the numbers of women who feel comfortable in being able to admit openly the exploitation or abuse they have experienced, but the numbers of men who have supported this campaign and are working to show that not all men are hardwired to oppress or to abuse their power and influence. Furthermore, the work of the actress Emma Watson with the #HeforShe movement has allowed many men to openly campaign for and support the rights of women, a topic that in previous generations was limited primarily to feminists.

Many millennial males choose to act as LGBTQ+ allies in their corporate environments and also support projects designed to include. For the millennial male, there is no inherent view that one group is in some way superior to another, or that society is regressing when the rights of women, the LGBTQ+ community or those from a minority black and ethnic background are being championed. Both views are still held by many men from previous generations.

As millennial males recognise their vulnerabilities and weaknesses, and become more self-aware, they also value and appreciate activities and programmes that help them develop and grow. The explosion of programmes to improve the mind or body, books that give self-help advice to men, the rise of mindfulness as a concept and a willingness to connect and converse with other men through initiatives such Men's Sheds (menssheds.org.uk) shows a growing desire by men to aid their own quest for fulfilment and growth.

It wouldn't be right of me to talk about the 'new masculinity' without a nod to the reference I made earlier about the 'new femininity'.

Millennial females are also experiencing a change in their values and expectations because of changing social norms, and this is impacting on how millennial males behave. It is argued that society is experiencing the fourth wave of feminism, which is one not driven by the label of feminism but by strong, influential women seeking to create practical solutions to overcome the barriers and challenges that still exist for women. For example, we know that women now have easier access to the workforce and can choose to work full time and move in to senior positions if they so wish.

The reality of this is, however, far behind the theory: there is a significant gender pay gap in many occupations, and many industries do not have a woman at the top of the organisation, none more so than in the FTSE100 where only seven women are in the top seat. The Institute for Chartered Secretaries and Administrators discovered that there were more chief executives called John in FTSE100 firms than there were women.

The new femininity stresses that there is no trade-off between being intelligent, powerful and feminine. Millennial females are just as likely as any previous generation to demand old-fashioned courtesy and respect from their male counterparts, not on the grounds of some sort of deference, but on the grounds of equality and the value of mutual respect.

Men who think that they are no longer able to compliment a millennial woman or hold a door open for her without being labelled oppressive or sexist are fundamentally missing the point. The new masculinity and the new femininity are complementary – they are underpinned by mutual respect and shared values. No longer is it acceptable to hold the door open for a woman, or carry a box for a woman because she is a 'delicate flower who needs a man's protection and strength', but it is acceptable to hold a door or offer to carry a box because it is common decency and courtesy that should be afforded to everyone irrespective of their gender, sexuality or ethnicity. Whereas the old masculinity and femininity was based on power imbalance and stereotypical judgments, and was conflictual, the new masculinity and femininity is based upon respect and equality and is consensual.

However, my chapter title refers to a sense of expectation. If everything is so consensual and equal, then why would millennial males feel a sense of expectation or any pressure? It is because the very nature of what it is to be a male and a female in a millennial age is changing that there is some friction between what we have been brought up to think a male should be, and what we know we should be based on what we sense is right.

Social media and influencers don't always help. Increasing numbers of photos and images projecting success, health and wealth for men seep out of every social media platform. Magazines filling the shelves at the local shop project images of men with abs, muscles and winning pearly white smiles, or in sharp suits and expensive watches, looking out to sea, where their boats are moored, while beautiful females hanging on their arm gaze lovingly.

I don't know about you, but as I swipe through the photos on Instagram, I look at myself and feel bad for choosing not to run every day, for choosing not to get up at 5am to get to the gym for exercise and the obligatory gym-selfie. As I thumb through the magazine in the shop, I look at my watch and my suit and wonder if I ever would afford these items. It is at this point that I generally get on my high horse and say that it is materialistic, that someone should not be judged on their six pack or the watch they wear, but on the quality of the person's soul. I generally feel better at that point, but am still left with a feeling that I am one of the minority who is not pushing hard enough, or fast enough.

The truth is that most millennial men are currently the primary earner in most circumstances and are under pressure to achieve, to work hard, and to live a lifestyle that is healthy, wealthy and successful.

Not got that promotion yet?

Not got that pay rise that you hoped for?

Not started that business yet?

Not moved out of home yet?

Not had your big break yet?

Not found the person of your dreams yet?

Not travelled the world yet?

Not got that six pack yet?

On and on, the questions implied by a society obsessed with success according to its various definitions play on our minds. The difficulty also comes when we still can't quite get rid of the hang-ups from previous generations about what a man should be.

We are asked to be sensitive and vulnerable, but not to the point where we are soft or lacking strength.

We are required to be less competitive and more accepting of failure, but we still chastise those who lack ambition or who have experienced business failure.

We are told that people should be judged on what is in their hearts rather than on their looks, but we still swipe left if someone doesn't look attractive to us physically, forcing us to be more aware of what we eat and how much we exercise, without developing the thing that will last the duration of our relationships: our character and personality.

We want to appreciate women, to compliment them and to act like the gentlemen that our mothers brought us up to be, but we are worried that might come across as our attempting to push a second wave of patriarchy, so we avoid doing it all together.

Globalisation has also impacted more on men, particularly working-class men, than on women. Roles traditionally occupied by working class men have gradually disappeared, making it harder for these men to gain access to new industries and occupations. While there is a push to encourage girls to study science, technology, engineering and mathematics and pursue careers in these disciplines, there isn't the same push for men in humanities and languages.

Sociological studies have shown that historically girls were pushed towards humanities subjects and had their work judged for neatness. This wasn't the case for boys. As society focuses on equality for girls in the classroom and the workplace, there is little evidence that boys are being encouraged actively to undertake study in subjects and train for careers that were once seen as the preserve of women.

There are still disproportionately lower numbers of men working in social care, for example, and our primary schools in the UK still face a crisis in recruiting male teachers. Some people still make assumptions about men who want to work in these environments, and that is something that the millennial generation – male and female – has yet to tackle with the same commitment as we do with regard to girls entering finance, science or technology careers. Millennial males are not being encouraged to transition to other roles that have historically been carried out by women; this runs the risk of stalling true equality in our workplaces and communities.

The pressure to be successful, to provide, to look good, to constantly be 'progressing' and developing are clearly some of the causes of poor mental health in the millennial male cohort.

I had been on medication for a 17-month period after being diagnosed with moderate depression in January 2017. My story is no different from those of many millennial males.

I made a decision in late 2016 to change careers and try something new – still a senior leadership role, but less well remunerated, which required an intense training programme that was pass or fail and would take me outside everything I had learned before.

Suffice to say, the career choice was not great. I didn't do my best work and struggled with some aspects of it. I resented not having the income, influence and ability to effect change that I had enjoyed in my previous role, and I missed the camaraderie that a medium-sized, family-run business can provide. I didn't enjoy the study or the assignments, I didn't like the style of leadership above me and, to be frank, I wasn't particularly good at the role. However, I felt stuck – unable to leave, as I had financial commitments, afraid to say to people that I wasn't up to it, and worried that I wouldn't find a suitable role to rejoin my old career.

So I said nothing, and pushed on. Each week became more difficult and challenging. Each month gave way to another of resentment and despondency, and I felt that I could not share my concerns with anyone, so I suffered alone. Peers around me seemed to enjoy their roles and fitted in well, using social media to post, adding to my sense of isolation.

I felt like a failure.

Eventually, I plucked up the courage to visit my GP. After an assessment, he identified that I had moderate depression, and gave me my first prescription for a drug called Mirtazipine (note to the reader: the label clearly states not to take it with alcohol. Trust me: follow that advice).

I wasn't sure whether to take the medication, but I did. It took me another 6–8 months before I was comfortable about telling people that I had depression, that I wasn't Superman (although I do look a bit like Clark Kent) and that I needed to make changes to my life to restore balance. I recently posted about it for National Mental Health Week on my social media and that was the first time that people outside my immediate family or friendship group knew anything about it, such was my feeling of shame and inadequacy.

It was a journey that forced me to be vulnerable and self-aware and to finally make the improvements necessary to help me get my life back. I left the job I hated, I gave up the time-consuming 'hobby' that had stopped being fun and was more of a chore, I spent more time with family and friends, and I finally made the life-changing decision to go into business for myself, something that I had wanted to do for a long time.

As I write this book, I have been off my medication for 10 months and I feel more energised, more in balance and control, and more fulfilled as a person.

The reason I tell this story is to show you that if you are struggling with the weight of pressure and expectation, it is worth seeking help and advice. As the now famous saying goes, 'It's OK to not be OK'. The moment that I – a millennial male with all the stress of life, the pressure to conform and achieve, and to be the best me for everyone else – recognised that I was struggling to keep afloat, was when I knew that I needed to take a series of small steps towards owning my condition, seeking help and allowing myself to be vulnerable and to be supported by others who loved and cared for me.

The incidence of male suicide and suicide attempts is too high. Too many millennial men are suffering as they valiantly try to be all things to all people. We need to recognise this – to encourage them to talk openly, and to offer a strong support network to help men navigate the crisis between old masculinity and the new.

You don't need to be superhuman.

You don't need to be perfect.

You just need to continue being you.

CONCLUSION

This book is not designed to be the be-all and end-all of books about the millennial generation; it was created to start discussing some of the key issues facing millennials as they accede to the mantle of being the largest generation alive by number across the globe.

I have deliberately avoided much conversation about digital technology as this is covered to death by other books and articles. Instead, this book is about advancing the conversation about who millennials are. The negative connotations associated with the word 'millennials', as though it were a dirty word, have led many people to avoid labelling themselves as millennials for fear of the judgment that it might bring.

Being a millennial is as much a way of being and thinking as it is the date on your birth certificate. Millennials are complex, driven by a desire to achieve and progress rapidly, but also by a want to make the world a better and different place from the one they inherited. The world we entered is debt-laden, insecure and still obsessed with categorisation: by class, age, gender, sexuality, ethnicity. The world we inherited is still shaped largely by a scarcity mentality: for me to win, you must lose – one only has to look at the rise of populism to see this. For millennials, this is madness, as their mindset is one of abundance: we can both win; there is enough for everyone.

It is why millennials are at the forefront of using technology to reshape relationships, to solve global and local problems and to try to create a world that is more about the character of the individual and not the label that has been affixed to them.

It is why millennials are impatient. Change needs to happen and happen more quickly than in the past, when people saw progress as something that should be gradual and accommodating of the status quo. This is insanity for a millennial: if you see something unfair or unequal, why would you not try to change it rapidly?

It is why millennials are focused on continually learning and developing.

> Why does knowledge need to come from on high?

> Why isn't it acceptable to look something up on Google or watch a YouTube video and then start applying it?

> What is wrong with trial and error?

It is why millennials are prepared to be more open, vulnerable and self-aware. For a millennial, each party should come to work, a business, a project or a relationship recognising that there will be imperfections, mistakes and error. Being open and honest is infinitely preferable to being right all the time. Relationships may be more fleeting and have more breadth, but networks and connections that are fluid and international enable millennials to pick up and put one another down as and when needed, rather than feeling obligated to deep relationships with everyone. We may have more Facebook friends, but we still value and revert to a small, deep pool of true and ever-present people for support and guidance.

It is why millennials are comfortable about airing their personal lives, their successes and their struggles. Everyone succeeds, everyone fails, everyone hurts, celebrates, struggles and achieves – so why not champion and support others? You don't need to be on personal talking terms to promote and empower people you come across in the offline or online world. Giving out compliments and making people feel intelligent, funny, attractive, successful or filled with potential isn't something to keep for a reserved bunch of special people: it is a gift to share with as many people as possible; for when we do it to others, they are likely to do it in turn to us when we need it.

Millennials get that.

Before I receive all the obligatory letters, emails, tweets and posts telling me that these qualities can be found outside the millennial generation, I get that, and I partially agree with you. However, this generation has these qualities by the bucketload. They don't need to practise them consciously, unlike others, because they already possess these qualities and naturally display them. It is what makes them different from other generations in mindset and approach, in the same way that members of generation X had their own natural qualities that baby boomers did not, and so on.

The Age of the Millennial is fast approaching. The world needs to be altered radically to meet the desires, dreams and aspirations of a very different generation, and this book is designed to help start that conversation; to help clarify what makes someone a 'millennial'; and to urge millennials, no matter where they are, to reclaim the positive aspects of being one, and to challenge all the assumptions of previous generations.

If you don't want to go to university, don't. There are other options!

If you can't afford your own home, don't panic. Renting is perfectly acceptable!

If you don't want a particular type of relationship, don't have one. Be with whomever you want, whenever you want!

If you want to work in a different way and want to hold out for an opportunity that best fits your own priorities and values, do that. The right opportunity will come along!

If you want to go straight into building your own business, stop watching all the podcasts and reading all the books about how others did it. Get on with it!

If you don't want to go into business just yet, go and experience a range of jobs and tasks. Get the necessary experience to give you confidence to strike out on your own!

If you want to compliment someone or hold open a door for them, do it. If you are doing it based on equality and respect, it is fine and should be encouraged!

Some of you will disagree with my views in this book, and that is fine. All I want to do is start the conversation and show you that there are other perspectives. If you are a millennial reading this book, you are living in a truly exciting time that is full of potential and opportunity. Make the most of it, create some clear plans, set yourself some audacious goals, tell the world about them, and go and make them happen. If we all do our bit to change our communities and our businesses to make them fit how we want to live our lives, the benefits will be enormous.

Your skills, qualities and attributes are exactly what the world needs right now.

Take action.

Claim your future.

Be proud to be part of the millennial generation.

ENDNOTES

1   The Sustainability Imperative: https:/www.nielsen.com/uk/en/
insights/reports/2015/the-sustainability-imperative.html

2   https:/www.theguardian.com/commentisfree/2019/mar/18/
jacinda-ardern-is-showing-the-world-what-real-leadership-is-sympa-
thy-love-and-integrity

3   https:/www.thelancet.com/journals/eclinm/article/PIIS2589-
5370(18)30060-9/fulltext - study can be found here

4   Taylor M, Marsh G, Nicol D and Broadbent P (2017). Good Work:
The Taylor Review of Modern Working Practices. London: Department for Business, Energy & Industrial Strategy

PRAISE FOR SEAN'S COACHING

"Sean takes the time to talk through ideas with his clients in detail. He is full of good ideas and works incredibly hard to ensure you implement them."

Simon Crowther, Director, Flood Protection Solutions Ltd, *Forbes* 30 Under 30 honoree

"I attended one of Sean's three-day Business Bootcamps and left feeling so motivated and focused on what I need to implement straight away in my own business, I have already started seeing results."

Nathan French, Director, Your Marketing Guy, former England Volleyball Captain and British Olympic Athlete of the Year, 2010

"Sean has helped me to build and develop my business from day one. He has held me accountable for all my actions and has pushed me to think differently about every day and the decisions I take in growing my company. Who knows where the company would have been if I hadn't met Sean, but one thing is certain, it wouldn't be anywhere near where it is today."

James Hardy, Director, Webink24

"When you think you have come to the end of the 'working on your business' phase, Sean ensures that there is plenty more work to do. I'd highly recommend him to any millennial entrepreneur seeking to grow their business."

Danny Marvan, Director, Marvans Tree and Landscapes

"At the turn of the year I knew that if I wasn't going to become part of the statistics that collapse within the first five years I need to get serious about what I was doing and, despite a great start, I knew there were lots of thing I was doing very naively, and a bit too much from the heart and not from the head.

"Sean has opened my eyes and encouraged me to start learning again. This has helped me on a journey of learning.

"We're a far more professional outfit now; we have the sales figures done every month and review financials weekly. We've got a far better grasp of our numbers and have come to grips with our values and culture. The most important thing I've learned about business is the importance of a vision and knowing where you're heading. Learning the reason why you're thinking five, and ten years ahead.

"Without Sean, my business wouldn't be where it is now. It's the accountability, as much as anything else, that's allowed me to push things on. It's about learning things, but then actually putting things around them and having a network of people who can help you along the way."

Rik Cridland, Managing Director, HayPigs!

"Six months ago, I met Sean to discuss some issues I'd had for a long time in my role as CEO of The Robin Cancer Trust. Within the first hour of meeting him I felt a clarity I'd been looking to find for years. I knew instantly that Sean's no-nonsense, no-excuses approach to coaching would be a good fit for the charity and me.

"Sean has transformed the way I approach my role – his style of coaching perfectly balances working through the six steps to business success with tackling real-time issues. This approach creates a recipe for immediate returns and long-term stability – something I think we can all agree we want for our businesses.

"Through Sean's Masterclass I have met a group of business owners, all from different backgrounds and sectors, all of whom share a similar aim – to reach their goals in business and live the life they dream of. This may sound like a marketing catchphrase (and no, Sean isn't paying me to say this!) but I assure I am much closer to making my goals a reality since joining Sean for the past six months, than I had been in the previous six years.

"I can't recommend Sean highly enough – through his coaching you will see a tangible structure to help you build your business, along with many intangible 'lightbulb moments' that will help you achieve your goals."

Toby Freeman, Chief Executive, The Robin Cancer Trust

"It has been great to watch Sean progress so quickly as a coach. His ambition, vision and belief was always there, and now he is backing this up with clear results, at fast pace and at a high level. We are very proud to have him as an ActionCOACH. Speed, instant impact on sales and marketing, self-belief and moving toward a positive future is how I would sum up what Sean does. Anyone fortunate enough to work with Sean will see the value of coaching translating into results quickly."

James Vincent, Performance Director, ActionCOACH UK

ABOUT THE AUTHOR

Sean Purcell is an award-winning business and leadership performance coach, speaker and trainer, based in Essex, UK. He has been referred to as 'The Millennials Coach' and is the founder of The Colchester Consulting Group, a strategy and operations consulting practice that works with businesses who want to work more closely with the millennial generation, whether as employees or customers.

He is also a certified business coach with ActionCOACH, the world's largest business coaching firm, and he works with business owners across the east of England to help them make more money, build better teams and create the lifestyles that they desire.

Sean has had a range of business experience, from owning a restaurant in the east of England, to being on the board of a multimillion-pound provider of outsourced public services. He has also sat on the boards of a membership association and a not-for-profit awarding organisation.

In addition to speaking and advising, Sean delivers one-to-one coaching and mastermind programmes for millennial entrepreneurs who have a five, six or seven-figure business and want to create the people, processes and products to take their business to the next level. His clients range from retailers to software, and many have grown exponentially because of his programmes. He also delivers three-day business bootcamps and is currently coordinating the first two-day, multi-speaker event for millennial entrepreneurs in the UK.

You can find out more about Sean and his projects by connecting with him here:

https://www.colchesterconsulting.com

https://colchester.actioncoach.co.uk

www.twitter.com/SeanPurcellAC

www.instagram.com/millennialssean

www.facebook.com/groups/themillennialscircle

www.linkedin.com/in/seanpurcellcoach